SEAHAM,
a
Town at War
1939 - 1945

Les Alexander

First published in Great Britain in 2002 by
Lighthouse Publishing
10 Glamis Road, Billingham, Cleveland,
TS23 2AA

All Rights Reserved. No part of this publication may be reproduced, stored in a retrieval system, or transmitted in any form, or by any means, electronic, mechanical, photocopying, recording or otherwise without the prior permission in writing of the copyright holder, nor be otherwise circulated in any form or binding or cover other than in which it is published and without a similar condition being imposed on the subsequent publisher.

c - Leslie Alexander, 2002

Printed and bound by C.O.S. Printers Pte Ltd, Singapore

CONTENTS

Introduction		v
Acknowledgements.		vi
Chapter 1.	1939 - The Phoney War and a time for preparation.	1
Chapter 2.	1940 - The gathering storm and possible invasion.	11
Chapter 3.	1941 - The tightening of belts.	35
Chapter 4.	1942 - Holding our own	47
Chapter 5.	1943 - Some optimism begins to surface.	69
Chapter 6.	1944 - 'And miles to go before I sleep.'	91
Chapter 7.	1945 - The end of the nightmare.	105
Chapter 8.	H.M.S. Seaham	113
Postscript		119
Bibliography		121

Introduction

At the time of writing it is over fifty years since the end of World War II and time has changed many things since those days.

The coal mines, so vital to the nation in 1939, no longer exist but the spirit of community that saw the best that human kind could achieve still thrives. That community overcame many hardships in the past and are making every effort now to build on what they have. These are proud people who value family and friends and take a great interest in the social and cultural activities in the area.

In writing this book I hope to enlighten those whose parents or grandparents lived through the days of armed conflict for there is a need to know among younger generations of where they came from and what was the stuff of those people in years gone by.

The following events are set in an almost diary like composition which I think gives a greater impression of the unfolding sequence of events and how people reacted to those events. I have included events that occurred in Murton as that township was also in the Seaham postal area. There are also included references to other areas where I felt that some events had a bearing on the people of Seaham.

Many friendships have been forged over the last few years with the good people of Gerlingen, Seaham's twin town in Germany and I trust that the reader will be aware that those people also lost loved ones in that war. There is always room to study a comparative history in situations such as this. Perhaps an account of life in Gerlingen during those years of conflict would be useful and would surely show us the futility of war.

L. Alexander B.A.,
August, 2001

This book is dedicated to my grandchildren,

Sam, Holly and Hannah.

May they inherit a world at peace.

Acknowledgements

As long ago as February, 1980 I began to look into an event concerning a crashed aircraft that I had known about as a boy towards the end of the war. I had many interesting letters about this event but the catalyst which sparked the ensuing research was a meeting with the late Bill Bulmer of Stotfold Farm. That meeting set me on the road to further research over the years seeking out source material for this book. I am indebted to Bill for that initial impetus.

I must also give special mention to other individuals, my friends Paul Jasper, (Worthing), Bill Brett, (New York), Brenda Thomas Bergerre, (Rome) Dr.Umberto Berrettini, (Rome), Rudolfo Borrani, (Stiava, Lucca), Tim Sheedy, (Red Deer, Alberta) Bert Gleave, (Blackpool), Kathleen Lawson, (South Hetton, Co. Durham), Dr. Trevor Williamson, (Hawthorn, Co. Durham) and also the late Joe Bragger, (Sheffield). Of course there were many others who lent their support and encouragement; to many to list here but they will know who they are. Thank you all.

Finally, I gratefully acknowledge the help and assistance given to me by the following:-

The Ministry of Defence, Air Historical Branch R.A.F. and Naval Historical Branch, The Royal Air Force Museum, (Hendon), The Commonwealth War Graves Commission, Imperial War Museum Department of Photographs, University Archives, Glasgow University, Durham Record Office, Durham Local Studies Centre, and Blandford House Records Department, Newcastle.

Chapter 1, 1939

The Phoney War and a Time for Preparation

This is the story of a town in the North East of England and of the people who lived in that town. Like many other communities at that time, they came together to wage war against Nazi Germany. Seaham was a hard working town, with enough problems of its own to overcome with poor housing and low paid, unacceptable working conditions in the coal mines.

As hard as life was, when war came in September 1939, the people were of one mind, to get on with the task and get it over with. There would be no quarter asked and no quarter given. Being a coastal town, Seaham always had a fair share of her sons serving in the Royal and the Merchant Navy and from the beginning of the war their numbers increased, together with many men joining the Army and the Royal Air Force.

On the Home Front, the miners did their bit by producing the coal that would be used in the making of steel for ships and tanks, guns and shells. There were sacrifices to be made and some loss of freedom but this was the only way to safeguard future freedom. Wives and mothers had the very important task of keeping the family fed and clothed, for much had to be done with scant resources.

Throughout August 1939, there was much talk of a coming war with Germany. Some thought that it would never happen others were sure that it would. Preparations were underway in Seaham to be ready in the event of war. At a meeting on the night of 4 August 1939, about 240 volunteer A.R.P. Wardens attended the Theatre Royal in Seaham and watched the Air Raid Precaution film 'The Warning.' At the start of the programme Coun. H. F. Lee, Chief Air Raid Warden, called for more volunteers to join the ranks because, if war came, it was best that Seaham should be ready. There was a need for a total of 340 A.R.P. men for the Seaham District. The casualty service was up to full strength as was the rescue and decontamination squad. The report centre and messenger group needed a further 32 volunteers.

The film, 'The Warning,' showed the different branches of the A.R.P. Service at work and how a local service could become proficient in their respective tasks. The manager of the Theatre Royal, Mr Harrison, a member of the Seaham Observer Corps, also addressed the gathering and expressed the hope that the people of Seaham would offer their services.

Britain and France had reaffirmed support for Poland but Hitler was mistaken in believing

Chapter 1, 1939

that if he attacked Poland then the French and the British would just stand aside; in any case, what could Britain and France do against the awesome might of Germany.

On the 1 September 1939, Germany invaded Poland and the British people held their breath. Surely this would mean war. Two days later, on the 3rd September,1939, Britain and France declared war on Nazi Germany.

There had been some rain the day before and on this Sunday morning four small boys were making channels in pools on waste ground in front of Mr Bird's chemist shop in Jubilee Avenue, New Seaham. A group of elderly men was standing at their usual meeting place by the high walled garden at the south end of Mount Pleasant. One of the small boys noticed that the men were looking skyward and, on looking up, saw puffs of smoke high up in the sky. "Bombs," cried one of the other children and they all scattered and made off for home.

The puffs of smoke were thought to have been practice anti aircraft gun firing out to sea.

Within a minute the air raid warning siren was heard throughout Seaham. However, some people who had been to Sunday morning church service, on leaving the church, were surprised to learn that the siren had already been sounded.

Mr Chamberlain, the Prime Minister, had announced Britain's entry into the war that morning but the sounding of the air raid warning so soon made many of the townsfolk more than a little apprehensive. However, when the 'all clear' note was heard there was general relief. The incident had proved that the A.R.P. Organization was ready for any emergency and, apart from the initial fright, the local units were quickly deployed.

There were twenty brick surface shelters already under construction in various parts of the town which would hold about fifty people in each as well as a public air raid shelter in the basement of Cliff House, which was now ready for immediate use. Three fire stations had been set up, one at Seaham Harbour, one at Dawdon and the other at Deneside.

Seaham Urban Council held a meeting the following day to appoint a Food Control Committee, as instructed by the Government. This committee was made up of ten members of the Council and five representatives from various trades people in the town and included G. W. Webster (butchers) W. Lightle (grocers) A Snowdon and T. McNee (other traders) and also the manager of Seaham Branch of the Co-operative Wholesale Society. A house in Bath Terrace was taken over as the offices for the Food Control Service.

Plans were submitted by Durham County Education Committee to build school air raid shelters that would house more than 3,000 children. These plans were approved and the Education Committee was asked to move as quickly as possible to get the building work underway. It was also suggested that, perhaps, the public might be allowed to use these shelters outside of school hours. Dr C. J. Neilan was put in charge of the first aid service in the area assisted by Mr Judd of Dawdon and Mr Ferguson of Seaham Colliery as first aid lay instructors.

The Phoney War and a Time for Preparation

Though the war was on everyone's mind at this time life had to carry on as normal and so, on 16 September, Miss Elsie Noble and Mr J. W. Walton were married at Seaham Parish Church. Perhaps this was not the best time to start married life but then Hitler was not going to be allowed to spoil the happy day.

There was some dissatisfaction from some quarters when it was learnt that A.R.P. Wardens were being paid £2 a week even though some of them had full time paid jobs. The wife of a serviceman complained that she was only getting 17s per week while £2 per week was being paid to A.R.P. Personnel even when there was more than one worker living in the house.

The 'blackout' was causing problems throughout Seaham, as it was all over Britain. One of the first casualties brought about by the blacked out streets was Mr Harry Elliot, of Dawdon Crescent, Seaham. He was knocked down by a car as he was crossing The Avenue. Two air raid wardens on patrol, D. Weatherall and A Temple, contacted the Control Room of the ambulance service and soon had Mr Elliot taken to Sunderland Royal Infirmary. There was another accident that same night when Mrs Elizabeth Frost, of Doctor Street, was knocked down on the Mill Inn Bank. Three wardens assisted in getting Mrs Frost to hospital as soon as possible.

One of the greatest problems that was coming to the surface was the spreading of rumours. Though government warnings about listening to and spreading rumours were published on posters and in the newspapers there were still rumours that went the rounds in pubs and clubs. One such rumour was the claim that Lord Londonderry had been interned. This untruth was quickly rejected. "Because I have entertained Von Ribbentrop and Goering, this did not make me a spy and a traitor", said Lord Londonderry.

While large public gatherings had been band at the outset the relaxation of this rule came about for football fans when matches were allowed to go ahead, starting on Saturday 30 September. Even so, matches were only allowed to be played on Saturdays or holidays. On this Saturday, Seaham White Star played Sunderland Corporation Electricity Undertaking and Dawdon C.W. took on Easington Colliery in the first round of the County Cup.

Identity cards were being issued at this time and holders were being told to take great care of them because, if they should get lost, a replacement would cost the holder 1s. Cards would have to be produced if a policeman should ask to see it or, if the holder had forgotten to carry it with him, then he would have to produce it at a police station within two days. No one in Seaham wanted Identity Cards, they were seen as a bother to carry around everywhere but there was a war on and this added inconvenience was generally accepted.

At the beginning of the month of September, an incident occurred one night after the pubs had closed which, though not to be condoned, shows something of the depth of feeling that was being felt by many towards Hitler. The incident occurred outside a pub in Church Street when a man who lived in South Terrace, Seaham, assaulted another man from Adolphus Street. In court, the defendant said that he and some other men were standing in Church Street talking about the war and he said that he would like to get his hands on Hitler. Just at that moment another man joined the group and said, "I'm Hitler", "So, I hit him", said the defendant. The man was found guilty of assault and bound over in the sum of 40s to keep the peace for twelve months. On a further charge of damaging the other man's false teeth, he was ordered by the Chairman of the Bench, Mr Malcolm Dillan, to pay £1 10s damages.

On 17 October, at about 1.55 p.m., the first real taste of war came with air raid warning sounding in the district. A single German aircraft had been spotted off the coast heading north. A.R.P. Wardens performed their duties well with a very good turn out. Streets were cleared quickly and all traffic stopped. The street shelters were well used by the public with no reported problems.

The fear of gas attacks was very real at this time and gas helmets for babies were being distributed by women wardens who had been trained in this work. They visited each house that had registered a baby and showed the mother how to use the helmet. The mother was then asked to repeat the demonstration to make sure she knew the correct procedure. She also had to sign for the gas helmet and promise to take care of it as each helmet cost £2-5s.

Men at Seaham Colliery formed an A.R.P. Unit at the pit and all those men were now fully trained. The control room was set up in the colliery office in a gas proof room that was sandbagged to protect it from bomb blast. This post was manned day and night and a small cabinet housed the air raid warning control. A telephone call from Sector would give the warning and a leaver in the cabinet would be pulled to start up the siren. In the cabinet there was also a red light and a green light. During the air raid or threatened air raid, the red light showed continuously while the green light flashed intermittently. When the 'all clear' note was sounded the red light would be extinguished and the green would show continuously. There were 16 fire fighters at the colliery and these were equipped with a fire trolley that contained a manual pump, hose and protective clothing and other appliances. This equipment was kept at the fire station, which was near to the colliery stables.

During the 14 and 15 October, there were heavy seas pounding the shore at Seaham and much of the cliff face was undermined. A house and a shop that had been built on the cliff top just sixteen years earlier by Mr J. Joiner, collapsed. Concrete slabs in front of the shop had given way and had fallen onto the beach so Mr Joiner abandoned the premised just in time.

There was bad news for the town on the morning of 14 October, when it was learnt that the British battleship 'Royal Oak,' had been sunk by a submarine in Scarpa Flow with the loss of over eight hundred young men. Seaham suffered four bereavements in this naval disaster and those who died were all between nineteen and twenty two years old. George Watson, 19, of Maria Street, had worked at Dawdon Colliery until 1938 when he joined the Royal Navy. John Hayes, 22, of Hall Street, had worked at Seaham Colliery since he left school. He joined the ship's company in June this year as a First Class Stoker. Frank Green, 20, of Ropery Walk, was a miner at Seaham Colliery before he joined the Royal Navy in 1937. Joseph Miller, 19, of Long Newton Street, Dawdon, had worked at Dawdon Colliery until he was sixteen and then he joined the Royal Navy. He had served in the 'Royal Oak' since June. Seaham people were left in a state of shock and sadness at this news so early in the war.

Children started to return to school on Tuesday 24 October after seven weeks of absence. A group system of attendance was brought in pending the provision of air raid shelters. The number of children affected was 4,758 and groups of forty children could attend school where there was accommodation for 200, sixty at schools where there was accommodation for between 200 and 300 and eighty children could attend their schools where the accommodation figure was more than 300. The scheme was voluntary and parents were asked to sign an undertaking to accept responsibility for the safety of their children. It was hoped that the children would attend at least two sessions per week but they were not allowed to attend school if they came without their gas masks. Once school shelters were fully available then it was hoped that normal school attendance would be operational.

At a council meeting that Tuesday evening concern was expressed by Mr W. P. Smith that during the air raid warning on the 17th a dispatch rider set out with the keys to open up a shelter and they were opened up immediately the keys came to hand. This was to slow.

Remembrance Sunday was observed at Dawdon Parish Church on 5 November. Among the large congregation were relatives of Joseph Miller and Frank Green of Dawdon parish. The loss of these young sailors touched the hearts of all those present. Over 500 people attended the Remembrance Day Services at Seaham Harbour Parish Church. A large number of Civil Defence personnel were present together with members of the Urban Council and Seaham and New Seaham branches of the Royal British Legion. The service at New Seaham was held in the afternoon at Christ Church and floral tributes were laid on the War Memorial in the Recreation Ground.

In the first week of November, a Murton teacher put on a display at the Warden's Post in the Old Schools, a model of Murton that gave a bird's eye view of all the streets and churches and other buildings in the area. The model would aid in the planning of routes and make mapping much easier. Wardens' posts in Murton were given names from the First World War such as 'Vimy Ridge,' 'Dicky Bush,' and 'Winnock.'

A letter arrived on the 14 November at the home of Mrs Richardson of Seaham Street, from her soldier son serving with the British Expeditionary Force in France. He wrote to tell his mother that he had found the grave of his father who had been killed in action during the First World War. Though Mrs Richardson had been informed of her husband's death and received his medals, his grave was unknown. Within the letter was a pressed flower that Private Richardson found by his father's grave.

At a meeting at Murton on Friday evening 17 November, councillors agreed to send a resolution to Mr Shinwell M.P. and to the Food Control Committee asking for an immediate rationing scheme for butter and bacon, etc. As these commodities were now in so short supply it was thought that rationing would give a fairer distribution of those scarce foodstuffs. Also, there was a call to have a price control put on such items in an effort to stop some traders who might be tempted to profiteer from the shortages.

There were air raids on Monday and Tuesday nights, 20 and 21 November, when German planes made reconnaissance flights over the East Coast. Fortunately on this occasion no bombs were dropped.

There was a drive to save paper at this time and Seaham Scout Group were taking on the task of collection. A two-wheeled cart was trundled around the streets at weekends collecting any waste paper that anyone had. The Girl Guides also did their bit in volunteering their time and efforts in many ways. The Guide Movement in Seaham was started by Miss N. Dillon in 1911, when with eight local girls, the first Girl Guide group was formed. At first they met in the nursery at Dean House then moved eventually into porpose built headquarters in the garden of Dean House.

Many Guides were now doing work of national importance. Some had taken their Gas Course and others were working for civil defence as typists, clerks and messengers.

On Tuesday night of this week, Mr W. P. Smith, Chairman of the Health Committee, raised the problem of the large amount of unfit meat that was coming into the town. He said that month after month his officials were finding unfit meat and that action should be taken to put the matter right. Councillor J. C. Jennings pointed out that the problem was not widespread but agreed that month by month it was the same names that came up in breach of health regulations. There was a suggestion that the appropriate authorities should be approached to see if a central depot for the slaughtering of cattle could be set up in Seaham. It was felt that Seaham was a big enough town to have its own abattoir.

Seaham branch of the W.V.S. was getting down to the task of providing comforts for servicemen. With donations of over five pounds they were buying wool to be knitted up into all manner of warm and comfortable things. Other articles were received from members of the public, one double sized quilt, four single quilts, two knitted woollen blankets, thirty-two blankets made up of squares knitted by volunteers, three pairs of operation stockings and twenty-four pairs of bed socks. This branch of the W.V.S. had adopted a military unit housed in a field opposite the gates to Seaham Hall and a number of parcels of such comforts had been delivered there; there were more to come.

The Town Council gave the use of an empty house for storing waste paper and the Scouts were busy collecting this. Mr Malcolm Dillon had asked for a systematic collection programme as the work was of vital importance and the Scouts were well placed to carry out this work.

The Murton Womens' Working Party, representing 28 organizations, co-ordinated a fund for comforts for Murton men who were in the forces. The Murton Mining Federation had already set up a weekly levy of 1d per head that raised about £10 per week. The same 1d levy was also asked of all trades unions, teachers, colliery officials, Northern General Transport and the Bakery and Co-operative Stores staff.

The War Services Committee at Murton met on 13 December and were told that 230 parcels had been dispatched and that 70 more were ready to go. Each parcel contained a pair of socks, a woollen helmet, a pair of mittens, cigarettes, sweets and a Christmas card. The value of each parcel was about seven shillings.

The Dawdon Workmens' Soldiers and Sailors Comforts Fund, headed by the miners' lodge was well under way. Mr T. Williams, a member of the committee, said that it had been suggested that a 1d levy should be introduced but it was felt by the majority that this would not be appropriate. He pointed out that Dawdon miners had many calls on their pay deducted at source and that a voluntary principle to raise funds would be best. The miners were subscribing all year round to hospitals, welfare schemes, aged miners' homes and treats for aged miners.

Though the scheme initially was to provide comforts for Dawdon miners now serving in the forces it was the intention to extend the scheme to others who had not worked at the pit. Dances and whist drives became a great source of raising money and there were Sunday night concerts in the Miners' Hall the first of which was held on the night of 10 December. This was a grand event organized by Mr Joseph Reed and his party from Deneside who delighted an audience of about 800 people.

One of the ways of listing all those who were away in the forces was the introduction of an envelope scheme. These envelopes were distributed to every household in Dawdon with the request for a donation. On one side of the envelope there was a space for the name and address of anyone in the household who was now a serviceman. In this way the committee could draw up a true register so that parcels could be made up and despatched.

Though expected air attacks over Seaham had not yet come about there had been air battles over the North Sea. In October, a lone Heinkel was making sweeps up the north-east coast on a reconnaissance mission to seek out the cruiser H.M.S. Hood which was believed to be in the area. About nine miles east of Whitby, the Heinkel was intercepted by three Spitfires from R.A.F. Catterick and the enemy aircraft was shot down some ten miles further east while trying to make its escape.

On Tuesday 12th December, the A.R.P. held a casualty practice in Seaham. Twelve 'casualties' were picked up by ambulance in different parts of the town and taken either to the first aid party depot at Dawdon Parish Hall or to the first aid post at New Seaham Parish Hall. They were treated for various 'injuries' by the well trained volunteers and overseen by Dr R.J. Hetherington and Dr C.J. Neilan.

As Christmas drew near there was a call from the Mission to Seamen asking the people of Seaham to be generous and give small gifts and Christmas cheer. An attractive programme was set up so that any seaman entering the port would be given a warm Christmas welcome. Many gave their time freely to bring the spirit of Christmas to those seamen who would be away from their homes at this time. Mrs Malcolm Dillon opened a Christmas Fair held in Dawdon Parish Hall on 13 December. Within an hour, Mrs Dillon was opening a Sale of Work at the Salvation Army Hall in Seaham Harbour. This busy lady commented that she felt like the fifth wheel on a coach as all the really hard work had already been done over the past months by dedicated church workers.

Another Christmas event was a non-stop review arranged and produced by Mr Fairless Wilson, in Murton Miners' Hall. Again, the £15 profit from this show was handed over to

Chapter 1, 1939

the War Services Committee Fund to provide comforts and cigarettes for Murton men and women who were serving their country. Christmas parcels were sent to each Murton man and woman in the forces, achieving the objective of the Murton Womens' Working Party in record time. There were 230 parcels sent which included 5 parcels for women. Each man received a pair of socks, a Balaclava helmet, a pair of mittens, cigarettes, sweets and a Christmas card. The parcels for the five women contained a scarf, sweets, handkerchiefs and a Christmas card. This group of women had more parcels to get ready for sending in the New Year.

We can see that all manner of help groups were galvanizing themselves to raise funds and do all they possibly could in their war effort. In three or four months, they had awakened a spirit that would overcome any hardship in order to give a little comfort to those in the forces and let them know that they were being remembered by family, friends and neighbours.

Over the last few months the overcrowding in Seaham was being dealt with by the new housing estate of Parkside where the first 404 houses were being allocated. The Minister of Health had written to the Council asking for details of the final allocation with numbers, size, type and completion dates of the new houses. The beginning of the Parkside housing estate was underway but it was feared that house building would slow down while the war continued.

Christmas time was different this year. Carol singers, however, did venture forth on Christmas Eve and with the aid of a bright moonlit night sky, carried their Christian message to all parts of the town. There were some changes though but the festivities went on even if less than in other years. There was no Midnight Mass or Communion service at either Roman Catholic of Anglican churches because of the blackout. Both St. Mary Magdalen's R.C. Church and St. Cuthbert's R.C. Church had representations of the manger of Bethlehem. Father M.J. Haggarty preached a Solemn High Mass at St. Mary Magdalen's and Father Gits conducted Masses at St. Cuthbert's throughout Christmas morning.

Staff at Seaham Hall Sanatorium attended a service at St. Mary's Church, Old Seaham, on Christmas Eve and, at St. John's Parish Church a nine - carol Service was held. Large congregations attended services both at Dawdon Parish Church, where a Sung Eucharist was led by Rev. James Duncan and at Christ Church, New Seaham, on Christmas morning.

On the theatrical side, Seaham Amateur Operatic Society were busy during the week with final rehearsals for a series of concerts to be held during the winter in aid of war charities. These concerts, as well as the normal productions, were seen as a way of taking peoples' minds off the troubles of war, at least for an hour or two. The live shows produced by Mr Jack Hilton and conducted by Mr Stan Hunter were much appreciated by full houses at the Theatre Royal.

There was a uniformed wedding on Boxing Day when Mr John Harrison of Rutland House Tempest Place married Miss Kathleen Olive Hutton. Mr Harrison, who had been an assistant surveyor at Vane Tempest Colliery before the outbreak of war was now serving as an officer in the army.

The year drew to a close; over half of the year had been taken up with talk of the possibility of a war breaking out and since September, the certainty that we were at war with Germany. The community of Seaham accepted this and many groups such as the W.V.S., Womens' Working Parties, Trade Union Groups, Schools, Scouts and Guides and War Services Committees and also ordinary members of the public took up the challenge. None knew what lay ahead but the townspeople were ready to make even more sacrifices if that should be asked of them.

Chapter 2, 1940

The Gathering Storm and Possible Invasion

As from Monday 8 January 1940, the people of Seaham were only able to receive their food rations from their registered retailer on handing over the appropriate coupon, (No.1). Foods that were now rationed could only be purchased if the coupon for that particular food was surrendered in that particular week in which it related. The townspeople would now really have to cut back on things such as butter (quarter pound per week), bacon or ham (quarter pound per week) and sugar (three quarters of a pound per week).

In recognition of their successful training, Counc. H.F. Lee presented badges to 23 wardens from Group 'D' of Seaham A.R.P. Service. Those receiving the badges were J. Bell, L. J. Button, R. Collie, H. Cummins, H. Dinsdale, T. Hanlon, M. Heckles, E. A. Hunter, G. Crozier, N. Lowrey, G. McLelland, W. McCloud, C. McQuilliam, S. McGrgor, J. Pigg, E. Reay, W. Ranson, A. Redden, L. Rochester, G. B. Teasdale, M. Walker, J. H. Wicks and A. Wilson.

Because of shortages of commodities the cost of living was steadily rising. The miners were looking for a rise in their pay of around 1s 4d per shift in order to keep up with the cost of living. However, the Coal Owners felt that they could only offer 4d per shift for men and 2d per shift for youths. At the National Delegate Conference of the Miners' Federation, convened in London, this offer was rejected. There were other problems starting to show up in the coal industry, one of which was the distribution of coal overseas. A shortage of shipping was said to be the cause of the problem here.

The first week of the New Year saw the loss of two British ships although there was actually a drop in the tonnage lost recently. Over the last three weeks the tonnage lost totalled 15,000 tons whereas in the previous three weeks the total tonnage was 95,000 tons. German aircraft had reconnoitred along the East Coast this week and on Tuesday of this week murderous attacks were made on unarmed shipping off the Durham coast.

On Wednesday evening, the Seaham branch of the Royal British Legion held a New Year Party in the Workmens' Club at New Seaham attended by 180 members. Everyone enjoyed themselves and between games and dancing members were served tea and cakes.

Mrs F. M. Gilmore of 43 Frank Avenue, Seaham, led 33 women volunteers in the Seaham Red Cross, manning the First Aid Post at New Seaham. At the beginning of the war when air-raids were expected at any time the women manned the post day and night but as time went on and air-raids had not, as yet, caused any problems the women were able to standby in their own homes ready to take up their duties when the call came. Dr C. J. Neilan was the medical officer in charge of the post and was responsible for training and organization. Everyone had their own allotted duties in attending the casualties that might occur and hospital cases would be sent to the nearest general hospital.

On Monday 8th January, Mr Shinwell M.P. spoke at a meeting in the Miners' Hall, Murton. He told his audience that he had proposed the stocking of coal some time ago but the Government had not taken this up and after he had approached the Minister for Shipping and the Minister for Mines this action was now to be put into operation. There was a possibility that more coal would be transported by rail rather than by ships because of the shortage of ships. He said that it was a disaster that at the time like the present pits in Seaham and other areas should be laid off and miners put on to short time working. Speaking of the changes in Whitehall, Mr Shinwell said that he had nothing to fear from the Germans but, between the 'Brass Hats' and the Prime Minister, we could easily lose the war.

Murton Church Hall resounded to music and laughter on Saturday night, 13 January. The Dalton-le Dale Young Peoples' Club were holding a carnival dance in the hall and there was a very good attendance. Throughout the area there was an attempt to keep young people occupied with social activities of this kind because the blackout restrictions meant that young people could no longer go about freely as they had done before the war started.

The Church of England schools in Seaham were only open on a part time basis because there were no school shelters. The Parochial Church Council applied for a faculty to have shelters built in St. Johns Churchyard. The shelters were to be built just inside the east wall of the churchyard and proper care would have to be taken to see that graves would not be affected.

By the middle of January, the Coal Owners offered an immediate rise of 5d per day on a cost of living basis. From the 1 January 1940, there would be a cost of living advance of .7d per shift for each point rise in the cost of living. There would be a three - monthly review and no further rise until the cost of living rose to five points. The miners had asked for an .88d per shift for each point rise but the Mine Workers' Federation Executive recommended that their members should accept this latest offer.

Money raised during the last Poppy Day Appeal in Seaham was forwarded to Capt. W. G. Willcox, Secretary to the Earl Haig British Legion Appeal. Mr J. C. Edington, Clerk to Seaham Council and District Organiser of the Poppy Day Appeal disclosed that the total amount raised was £124 1s 1d. The total for 1938 had been £113 11s 2d so, even with the present difficulties, the people in the town were prepared to dig ever deeper in their pockets to support this fund.

Winter came with a vengeance towards the end of the month with very heavy falls of snow. Miners gave up their time to cut out paths to Seaham Colliery so that men could get to their work. Many children could not get to school that day and those that did get to Seaham High Colliery School spent the day working at their lessons seated around roaring coal fires. All roads into the town were blocked and the railway lines were also closed.

In the first week of February, the people of the town had saved hard for the war effort by buying Savings Certificates to the value of £684, Defence Bonds of £50 and savings bank deposits of £177. Because of a shortage of the usual commodities there was not a lot to buy so money saved in this way was put to good use.

On Saturday 3 February, a number of Heinkel bombers, thought to be about thirty, launched what was perhaps the biggest raid on shipping in the North Sea. A British convoy was sailing south down the east coast and the 'Lion' Group of He111's was sent out from Schleswig in North Germany to attack. The Chain Home radar station at Danby Beacon picked up the strobe signals of the approaching aircraft and quickly verified that they were 'hostile.'

The warning was immediately passed to Sector Headquarters for action. As the convoy sailed past the coast off Seaham in a snow storm, some of the German aircraft made their attack, bombing and strafing the decks of the ships. A Halcyon Class Minesweeper, H.M.S. Sphinx, was hit and badly damaged, so much so that she capsizes while she was being taken in to port. This little ship had lost 54 members of her crew.

Because of the heavy snowfall some days earlier, there was only one fighter station, near Alnwick, clear of snow. It was up to three Hurricanes of 43 Squadron at R.A.F. Acklington to be scrambled and join battle with the enemy. They caught up with one of the raiders and it was soon overwhelmed by the fire power of the three Hurricanes. Badly shot up, the Heinkel made for land and crash-landed in fields north of Whitby; this was to be the first German aircraft to be shot down in England.

Eighteen years old Bernard Wilson of 60 Jasper Avenue, Deneside, arrived home this week after a thrilling adventure at sea. Bernard had been taken prisoner in the South Atlantic when his ship Steonshalk, out of Whitby, was attacked by the German Pocket Battleship 'Graf Spee.' This was on the 7 December and after taking to the lifeboats the German captain, Captain Lanngsdorff, ordered them to return to their ship to collect their blankets and eating utensils. The thirty - two crew were then taken on board the 'Graf Spee.'

Young Bernard and the rest of the men were quartered three decks down under the forecastle head and sealed in by a water tight door. Men from other ships that had been sunk by 'Graf Spee' had been transferred to a tanker in Montevideo and two of these men were thought to be Mr Ralph Miller of Hawthorn Square and Thomas Leighton of Rectory Cottage, Seaham. On the 13 December, in the early morning, the Graf Spee's three eleven inch forward guns began to fire, deafening the captives below. The Graf Spee was under attack herself now. A German Petty Officer confirmed to the prisoners that his ship was being attacked by H.M.S.Ajax and H.M.S.Exeter. Later in the battle H.M.S.Exeter was sunk.

After about two hours of firing and receiving hits, the Graf Spee's guns fell silent for a while and the prisoners below continued playing 'Nap' with matches. The running battle continued for most of the day. At about midnight, the battleship put into Montevideo and the next evening all of the prisoners were taken to the 'Sailors' Home' where they stayed about nine days before being sent back to England.

In almost two months of service the Graf Spee had sunk nine ships until the British cruiser squadron commanded by Commodore H. Harewood found her in the South Atlantic. Forced to break off the engagement because of the tremendous fire power of the battleship, the cruisers stood off the mouth of River Plate where the German ship had taken refuge. British Navy reinforcements were brought up and, on putting to sea again, the captain of the Graf Spee saw no escape and so scuttled his ship before taking his own life.

Mr A. G. W. Boggon gave a lecture on Sunday 11 February, to the young people of St John's Church. His talk was on the characters of Shakespeare and was very well received by about seventy youngsters. They later joined in community singing with Miss J. McKeith at the piano and J. Curry sang a solo. The following Wednesday evening saw another gathering of young people in the Church Hall, where Jack Wick gave a lecture on the songs and poems of Robert Burns. He followed this by singing a number of songs by Burns with Mrs Wick accompanying him on the piano. This was again followed by community singing. It was generally thought that these meetings would be a pleasant way for young people to get together socially during the dark days of winter.

The blackout was having a serious effect on going about their business at night. The people of Seaham were warned to take extra care when crossing the road as there had been 1,200 people killed in Britain throughout January alone and there had been many more injured. Considering the fact that there was much less road traffic than there is in the present day, this figure is horrendous.

On Sunday 18 February, in the very early hours of the morning, two Seaham merchant navy officers stepped out of a taxi in Seaham Harbour, free men again. Ralph Miller (22) and Thomas Leighton (32) had been prisoners in the German supply ship Altmark since their respective ships were captured by the Graf Spee, in the South Atlantic. The two men had never met before until they were taken on board the Altmark. Mr Miller had been a prisoner for seventeen weeks since his ship 'Ashlea' was sunk on 7 October last. Mr Leighton's ship 'Doric Star' was sunk on 2 December.

Eventually the Altmark docked in Norway and the prisoners had an idea that they were in Bergen and knew that there was some kind of search being made by the Norwegian authorities but, although they made much noise to attract attention, the only response was that the Germans put out the lights and turned the hose pipes on them. However, British Intelligence knew of the prisoners and when the Altmark was spotted by LAC Jack Sheekey flying in a Lockheed Hudson of 220 Squadron from Thornaby they sent the destroyer H.M.S. Cossack in with a boarding party. On the previous Friday night, the prisoners heard rifle fire but did not know what was going on until the hatch was opened and a cheery voice shouted down, "Are there any Englishmen here."

The Cossack made for home at once and the freed men were put ashore at Leith on the Saturday afternoon. After being medically examined in hospital, the two Seaham men set off for home.

The last train from Newcastle to Seaham had left so the two men took a taxi for the last dozen or so miles to their homes. Both men expressed their gratitude to the Commander, Officers and Men of the Cossack for their daring rescue. The flag of St. George flew over St. Mary's Church, Old Seaham, all day on Sunday in celebration of the return of Mr Leighton of Rectory Cottage nearby. Celebrations were going on in a house in Hawthorn Square also, where Mr Miller with his mother and father were receiving relatives and friends all day.

The freezing weather over the last few weeks had brought with it the problems of frozen and burst water pipes that resulted in a water shortage. The Council asked the locals not to swill down yards and footpaths and to save water wherever possible.

Mr J. G. Foggin, who had a newsagent shop in Church Street, was elected President of the North Eastern District of the National Federation of Retail Newsagents. Mr Foggin had been a newsagent in Seaham for forty years before the outbreak of war.

Meat shortages were causing many complaints at this time and it was because of this that the Government brought in meat rationing on 11 March. Each person was allowed a ration of meat to the value of 1s 10d per week. A shortage of shipping was said to be the cause of the shortages and rationing in this way would see that everyone would get a fair share of the available meat each week.

In Murton on Monday night 12 March, the Amateur Operatic Society began their new show 'The Desert Song,' that was to run for the rest of the week in the Rex Theatre. The profits from the show would go to the Comforts Fund. Fred Tindale as Pierre Birabeau alias 'Red Shadow' and Ester Barnes as Margot, held the first night audience in raptures with their love scenes and singing. The excellent cast made sure that the show was, as always, a great night of entertainment.

On the 26 March, Seaham Urban District Council met to consider the position of A.R.P. personnel who were miners. A letter had been received by Mr T. Scollen, Chairman of the A.R.P. Committee, from Mr F. Wilson, Manager of Dawdon Colliery, which suggested that miners should give up their A.R.P. work and return to full time work at their collieries. The need to increase coal production was now being made forcibly by the Government and Mr Wilson felt there was a greater need for the men to be working in the coal mines than in patrolling and protecting the citizens of the town from any possible air raid in the area.

There was some talk that if these men did not return to the pits then their jobs might not be held open to them. There was much concern that if the men did return to the pits then there would be a great loss of personnel in the A.R.P., 60% were miners, of the Auxiliary Fire Service 78% were miners. It was suggested that Londonderry Collieries Ltd. should be approached to stay their hand until the Council had some directive from the Home Office about the problem. If the Home Office confirmed that the men should return to work in the mines then the Council hoped that time would be given for the training of council employees to take over these services.

In J. B. Priestley's 'A New English Journey,' heard on B.B.C. radio on Tuesday 23

Chapter 2, 1940

April, Priestley interviewed three local men, Mr T. A. Mackey, manager of Vane Tempest Colliery, Mr Charles Ferguson and Mr Fred Henderson who also worked at Vane Tempest pit. It would seem that Priestley's visit to Seaham was hardly worth the trouble as there were many complaints from local listeners that the item from Seaham was far to short, compared with the visits to other parts of the country. Seaham was only 'on air' for two or three minutes as can be gauged from the broadcast dialogue.

Mr Mackey: "Good evening, Fred."

Mr Henderson: "Evening, sir."

Mr Ferguson: "Good evening. Are we going to make progress on the Maudlin Seam yet, Mr Mackey?"

Mr Mackey: "Well, we will when we get the men."

Mr Ferguson: "Aye, there's a canny lot of lads gone since the war started. Over 500 from the three pits, they were saying."

Mr Mackey: "Over 700 from the three and the best part of 250 from Vane Tempest alone."

Mr Henderson: "Wey aye, I've got a son in the Tank Corps myself and two sons-in-law out with him, one in the D.L.I. and the other in the R.A.F. There's three from one family."

Mr Ferguson: "Aye, there won't be a man left in Seaham the way we are going on."

Mr Mackey: "Well there's plenty on the reserve list, y'know, if they all stay. And we can't afford to be down on what we were getting out when the war started. And we could employ another thousand men and boys."

So, there it was, Priestley's visit to Seaham on B.B.C. Home Service. The discussion seems to have been designed to underline the need for more men to work in the coal mines around Seaham and to keep up production targets.

Miss M. Marriott gave a demonstration of 'Wartime Cookery' in Dawdon Parish Hall on the Wednesday afternoon of that week at a meeting of the Townswomens' Guild. Afterwards, Mrs A Elgey read out a letter she had received from the B.B.C. The Guild had sent to the B.B.C. suggestions on how to counteract the invidious broadcasts from Germany by William Joice, 'Lord Haw Haw.'

Jack Wick, the local tenor, was again busy on the Friday evening when he gave a lecture to the St. Hild and St. Helen's Black-out Club. His lecture this time was on church music and the president of the club, the Reverend James Duncan, thanked Mr Wick for a very interesting and enjoyable talk.

With men joining the forces now in ever growing numbers, there was becoming an acute shortage of manpower on the land. As food production was now vitally important a scheme was being put forward that would allow schoolboys to do work on farms. The scheme envisaged Summer Camps being set up where older boys, those over 16 years old, could go to help with farm work. Local farmers were advised that they should make payment of sixpence an hour to boys over sixteen years old and five pence an hour for those under sixteen. It was stressed that the boys must be insured while doing farm work and also insured while living in the Summer Camp.

The people of the town had the chance to lift their spirits a little by visiting the cinema for a good laugh at the beginning of May. At the Empire cinema the Marks Brothers were in great form in 'At the Circus,' said to be their funniest film over the last seven years. At the Theatre Royal, Ginger Rogers starred in 'Bachelor Mother,' where she finds an abandoned baby but her predicament is that she cannot convince anyone that the baby is not hers. Visits to the cinema were very popular and besides being entertained for a couple of hours or so, there was the chance to see newsreels of how the war was going though much of it was of a propaganda nature it gave the audience a positive outlook that was very important. There were also lots of Ministry of Food 'shorts' that would show people how to make the best of their weekly rations.

The old Vane Hall at Seaham had been turned in to a Soldiers' Club over the last few weeks, under the supervision of Capt. A. S. Banks. Doors were opened at 2p.m. and the club remained open until 10 o'clock in the evening. There were facilities provided for the writing of letters, with free note paper and there was a very good selection of books provided by the local community as well as magazines and morning and evening newspapers. The number of soldiers coming in from local barracks was increasing all the time. The club was busiest at weekends when soldiers had their afternoons free. For recreation there was a full sized billiard table and another smaller one, a dart board and some table games such as dominoes, draughts and chess. The billiard tables were probably the most popular.

One of the big attractions to the Soldiers' Club was, of course, the canteen where the servicemen could enjoy fresh home made sandwiches at a penny each and sausage rolls and cakes at a penny each. For drinks there was always tea at a penny a cup, coffee, malted milk and minerals. The canteen was run by about twenty ladies from the St. John's Parish Church Mothers' Union. Working in turns, they did two or four hourly shifts on a rota system. A number of men worked in the club in the evenings and many were from St. John's Mens' Fellowship. Townsfolk were very generous in setting up the club and provided gifts of furniture, a wireless set and even a gramophone and some records together with books, magazines and writing paper.

Vane Hall had been erected in 1862 as a drill hall for the 2nd Durham (Seaham) Volunteer Artillery Brigade and was in use by them until 1888, when the Drill Hall in Castlereagh

Road was built. Vane Hall later became a dwelling house until the death of the owner, when it became vacant.

Seaham people were told at the beginning of May that there would be no organised attractions at Crimdon during the Whitsuntide holiday because of the war. Though the beach would still be open and also the Dene, visitors would have to make do with the old fashioned picnic day out. Men in the forces this Whitsun were sent postal orders for three shillings as a Whitsun gift from the Seaham War Services Fund.

On Wednesday 15 May, 298 men volunteered to join the anti-parachute defence corps at a time when it was thought that a German invasion might be launched. In Murton, 400 men made the application to enrol as 'Parashooters.' Among these was ex-sergeant 'Billy' McNally, who was awarded the Victoria Cross and the Military Medal in the first World War.

Sad news came at this time that Gunner George Purvis of Dalton-le-Dale had been killed in action. George, who was twenty-nine years old, had formerly worked at Murton Colliery before the outbreak of war.

There was some confusion about the Whitsun Bank Holiday that was supposed to be cancelled this year but notice that it had been cancelled seemed to have been given to late as some shops opened as usual while others closed.

The first three groups of the Seaham Local Defence Volunteers (L.D.V.) - Unkindly named 'Look, Duck and Vanish' - began patrolling on Saturday night, 25 May. One group gathered on the cliff top at Seaham Hall under the supervision of a retired army major who had possession of one .22 rifle. He ordered the group to collect large pebbles from the beach ready to throw down on any invading German troops who might come ashore on Seaham beaches. The serious situation in France had brought home the real possibility of an invasion of the British mainland much nearer. Large numbers of people attended Seaham Harbour Parish Church on Sunday 26th, in a National Day of Prayer. Spirits were very low.

On 27 May, the evacuation of the British Expeditionary Force began at Dunkirk. Though it was thought that, perhaps, 100,000 men would be rescued from the shores of France in the event, by 4 June, about 340,000 were brought back, two thirds of them were British soldiers. Was this perhaps divine intervention brought about by the power of a National Day of Prayer?

A wire-haired terrier was made a member of the Observer Corps this week and had a special badge made for him. The dog's qualification for membership was his excellent hearing and that as soon as he heard an aircraft approaching, long before his owner did, he would begin to 'pant.'

The Police Courts in Seaham were imposing much harsher fines on people who had not obscured house lights properly. It was important that the slightest amount of light shining through carelessly fitted blackout curtain was rectified. Three people were each fined £1 on

31 May, which doubled the fines of the previous week when thirty people were fined 10s each.

At the same court on the following Monday, two alien seamen were fine £2 each for being ashore without permission. At 10.50 p.m. on Monday night of the previous week, P.C. Stephen was on duty near the docks at Seaham when he saw two men making their way towards the docks. He stopped the men for questioning and found that they were foreign seamen and so asked to see their permits. The two could not produce any permit and were charged with the offence. Mr G. Deans, Immigration Officer, said that the men, Stefan Kazula (18) Karl Lennart (17), should have applied to him for a permit but had not done so. Alien seamen were not allowed ashore without a permit and, in any case, even with a permit this would only be allowed between the hours of 6a.m. and 8p.m. Mr Malcolm Dillon (Chairman) told the Master of the foreign ship that he must inform his men that when they come to this country, they must obey the law.

On Friday 14 June, East Murton Parish Council decided to ask the South Hetton Coal Company if they could use land at the top of Wood's Terrace as a collecting point for scrap iron. Mrs M. Bolt was the organiser of the scheme and asked if anyone had scrap iron or steel if they would take it to this site to save time. There were collectors busy in this task but scrap metal was needed urgently so people were being asked to co-operate.

It was also disclosed at this council meeting that there were twelve organizations with 700 members in Murton and Cold Heseldon, contributing to the National Savings Scheme. National Savings was seen as one of the best ways of providing the funds to buy the war weapons needed to fight the enemy.

About the middle of June a letter arrived from the War Office at the home of Mr and Mrs McLoram of The Avenue, Seaham, telling them of the sad news of their son, Pte. Peter McLoram (21), who had been killed during the withdrawal from Dunkirk. Pte. McLoram was the first member of St. Mary Magdalen's Church to give his life for his country.

The phoney war ended for the people of the town when Heinkel bombers attacked on two successive nights, 19 and 20 June. The attack took place just after 11p.m. on the Wednesday night and the all-clear siren did not sound until about four hours later. There was some damage to property over the North east area and some loss of life.

This first contact with enemy aircraft caused quite a strong reaction from the civilian population. Instead of taking shelter during the raid many came out of their homes to 'take a look' at what was happening. Sir Arthur Lambert, Regional Civil Defence Commissioner said that people had not yet realized the risk from bursting bombs and he made four suggestions for future action.

(1) Remain in doors. Lie on the floor away from windows.
(2) Be sure the blackout is complete before putting on any lights.
(3) If caught outside, make for the nearest shelter but don't panic. If the shelter is too far away ask for admittance to the nearest house.

(4) If you live on the coast and troops of the enemy gain a foothold, stay indoors and await orders from the police or military.

He went on to say, "These things may never happen so carry on and show a cheerful countenance." This advice may sound a little melodramatic to later generations but in 1940 things were deadly serious and the people of Seaham were just getting to grips with the possibility of an invasion.

School children in the town were told of the new arrangements for attending school because of the air-raids that were taking place with increased regularity. The Director of Education, at a meeting of the Education Committee on Wednesday 26 June, outlined the new arrangements.. If a raid of more than one hour occurred after midnight then the morning session at school would be cancelled. If there was a raid during the day then school would be dismissed and if a warning was given but no raid took place in the morning and lasted long enough to interfere with the normal dinner hour then the afternoon session would be abandoned. The children might have thought these rules were a great idea but the effect on the progress of their education could not be measured.

Another topic for discussion was the use of school shelters by the general public. Alderman G. Blackwell said that, in Seaham, people had wanted the shelters to be opened to the public at night and on one occasion there had been a rush to a school shelter but it was locked and the key holder could not be found. He believed that when the school was closed the shelters should be locked and that the County A.R.P. Committee should be responsible for the provision of public air-raid shelters.

Sadness came to Murton in the first week of July when Mr and Mrs F. Smith were informed that their only son, Pte. F. Smith, D.L.I., had been killed in action. Pte. Smith (21) had worked at Murton Colliery before he joined the army after the war broke out. Better news arrived in a letter to relatives of Pte. Gabriel Hill of Murton, telling them that he was a prisoner of war in Germany. They had not had any news of him for some weeks until a letter arrived from the Swiss Red Cross telling them that he was a prisoner. A letter arrived on June 22 from Pte. Hill saying that he was quite well.

One family in Seaham was very proud of the commitment to the war effort of five sons. Mr and Mrs Thomas Barksby, of 102 Ash Crescent, Parkside, had five sons now serving their country in the forces, Sergeant George Barksby (40), Sapper Thomas Barksby (33), L.A.C. William Barksby (28) R.A.F., Signalman Fred Barksby (22) and L.A.C. Norman Barksby (19) R.A.F. The other sons were miners working at Vane Tempest and Dawdon Collieries.

On Friday 28 June, the miners of Seaham received their holiday credits. Patriotic to a man, they gave up their annual week holiday to work and produce yet more coal. Holiday pay was being paid to 2,400 at Dawdon Colliery, 1,700 at Vane Tempest and 1,600 at Seaham Colliery. Each married man received £2 12s, a single man £1 10s 4d and youths under eighteen £1 1s 8d. The total sum paid out including the normal working week's pay was £29,000. About 500 coal hewers at Seaham Colliery received an additional 2s 6d each from the weigh fund. About £300 was also distributed to the men from the Durham Miners' Gala Fund. Though it was not to be held this year, the men had already paid in to the fund.

Seaham Urban Council suggested at a meeting in the first week of July that the Russian gun that had stood on Terrace Green for more that eighty years, should be sent for scrap to aid the war effort. The inauguration of the gun on Terrace Green by Lady Frances Anne, Marchioness of Londonderry, was the subject of a painting that hung in the Londonderry Offices for many years.

Alarm was expressed in Murton that there were still not enough air-raid shelters. An appeal was made to the County Education Committee for the school shelters at the Council School to be opened to the public during an air-raid. The collection of scrap metal in Murton was going quite well by now but Mrs M. E. Bolt, the organiser, said that there was a need for more men to come forward to man the collecting cart.

An enemy aircraft dropped four bombs in the early hours of Sunday morning 21 July. They all landed in a farm field and exploded harmlessly even though there were fifty cows in the next field.

On 26 July, the people in the town learned that there was to be a new 'White Loaf' produced which would be more healthy than the white bread that had been available so far. The new 'White Loaf' was to be fortified with vitamin B1, which would help to see people through times of stress when every mental and physical effort was needed to win through.

Some of the air-raid shelters in Seaham were being damaged by children who were tending to use them to play in. Posters were put up to encourage children to respect the shelters and realize that they were there for a very serious purpose. There was also concern that some people were being premature in thinking that they should take to the shelters when the preliminary warning of an air-raid came through. This was just a precautionary warning received by the civil defence forces to man their posts and members of the public on seeing the services turning out were breaking their normal routine to make for the shelters. The townsfolk were advised that they should only take action when they heard the siren sound.

Juvenile crime was on the increase at this time, prompting comments from Mr Malcolm Dillan. He recalled that, in his memory as a magistrate, juveniles brought before the court were so few that their cases were heard at the end of normal court sessions and reporters did not bother to wait to hear cases of juveniles unless they were of a serious nature. Now cases had increases so much that there were regular Juvenile Court sessions. The charge sheets denoted a great increase in juvenile crime and at the last week's session no fewer than twelve children were before the court with an average age of twelve years old. Absence of fathers had been blamed during the First World War for the misdemeanours of young people but the present situation had not yet resulted in so many fathers being away from home.

At the Olympia Theatre on Saturday 3 August, Company Sergeant-Major Thomas Pallas, who had been awarded the Military Medal, was presented with an inscribed gold wristlet watch from the people of Murton. On 21 May, Sergeant-Major Pallas took his platoon, under heavy fire, towards their objective and captured a building that contained 25 German troops. At the time he was a sergeant and had since been promoted.

Sergeant-Major Pallas was among the B.E.F. forces that were able to get away from the Dunkirk beaches; he had gone without sleep for five days. The presentation of the watch was made by Murton's only V.C., ex-Sergeant Billy McNally, who won his V.C. in action on the Piave during the First World War.

The War Office this week reported that two Seaham soldiers had been taken prisoner. Lance-Corpral Charles Gale (21) R.A.S.C., son of Mr and Mrs John Gale of California Street, Seaham, had been in the army since last December and previously had been employed as a van driver for the Seaham and District Laundry. The other soldier was Private Richard Head Williams (37) A.M.P.C. of Queensbury Road, Deneside. He had been in the army for five months and after training went to France. Pte Williams father fought in the First World War and died of wounds received in action.

Mr E Shinwell, M.P. visited the area A.R.P. organisation on Saturday 10 August and was shown the wide range of equipment and facilities which the organisation now had in operation. He took particular interest in the provision of public shelters in the area. Mr Shinwell was responsible for the decision, taken by the Home Secretary, to provide shelters in non-specified areas and authority for the building of communal shelter for the public generally.

Over the last week there had been a number of air-raid warnings but the 'all-clear' siren had sounded without any enemy aircraft making an appearance. Of course, the 'Battle of Britain' was raging in the south of England and R.A.F. Fighter Command was being stretched to the limit. Some fighter squadrons had been sent north to rest up from the conflict that was going on in the South.

On Thursday 15 August, just before one o'clock the sirens sounded throughout the town and people quickly made for their shelter. Within a few minutes there were a number of Heinkel 111's overhead and the anti-aircraft batteries were opening up on them. There was a tremendous amount of noise from the aircraft, the shells bursting and bombs exploding. Shrapnel from the shells was flying about and rooks and crows from Dawdon Dene, frightened by all the noise, were circling over Parkside in terror.

These Heinkel bombers, the Lion Geschwader of Luftflotte 5 stationed in Stavanger, Norway, were escorted by twin engined Messerschmitt Bf110 fighters of the Zerstorer (destroyer) unit. There had been an attempt at a feint by He115c float planes to try and draw off the fighters of 13 Group but because of an error in their DR navigation the ploy did not work.

The Chain-Home radar station at Turnhouse reported the approach of the enemy bombers on vector 230 degrees and 13 Group Command scrambled 72 Squadron based at Acklington to go into the attack. Because this was the biggest air attack the North East had had so far, the radar operators were not experienced enough to judge accurately the number of bombers that were showing up on their radar screens. They reported about thirty in number whereas there were in fact seventy-two Heinkel 111's and twenty-one Messerschmitt Bf 110 fighters as escort.

The raiders came in near the Farne Islands and turned south. Seventy-Two Squadron passed over the enemy formation and about three thousand feet above them. As the British fighters flew east, a wing man called up his leader and asked, "Haven't you seen them?" "Of course I've seen the b-b-b-bastards; I'm trying to w-w-w-work out what to do." This message became a source of humour throughout Fighter Command.

Turning to attack out of the sun, the Spitfires made their run in and were then joined by Hurricanes of 49 Squadron, also from Acklington, 607 Squadron from Usworth and 605 Squadron from Drem in southern Scotland. Some of the bombers jettisoned their bombs and headed for home while others flew on. By the time the aircraft were over Seaham there was a general scatter because they were being harassed so much by the Spitfires and Hurricanes. More Spitfires from 41 Squadron based at Catterick also joined the fray.

A number of houses in Ilchester Street, Stavordale Street and Fenwick's Row, Seaham were hit by bombs during this attack and several people were killed. Four people in one house were killed and in the same street Mrs Shaw (56), a widow, was killed as was her married daughter Mrs Johnson (29). However, Mrs Johnson's eighteen months old baby survived almost unhurt. Also killed in the raid were Mrs Ferry (46) and Mr Edward Swan (35). A number of people had to be taken to hospital and these included Mr Henry Gale (25), Mrs Gale (22), Mr J. Harvey (29), Mr Patrick Brett (46), Mr Nicholas Brown (50), Mr Robert Bird, Mrs Elizabeth Kirby (30), Mr George Cummings (67), Mr John Ferry (16) and Mr Thomas Herrington (63).

In another street three houses were hit and it was here that Mr Swan and Mrs Tempest were killed. Mr and Mrs Dyson, who lived opposite, said that the door knocker, door knob, key and nameplate of one of the houses crashed through their front window and the curtains of the same house were blown into their passage. An air-raid warden, Mr Sample, out on duty, took cover behind a wall as there had not been time to reach his post before the bombs fell. He said that the noise of the explosions was terrific and clouds of dust and flying pieces of metal were everywhere. When the aircraft had moved off, the A.R.P. got right on with the job of looking after the injured and searching for survivors.

Dawdon Parish Church was damaged and a large hole was made in the north wall; the roof of the north aisle lost most of its slates. The vicarage, next to the church, was also badly damaged with ceilings down and many windows broken. There was also a large crater in the garden. The Vicar, the Reverend. James Duncan, on hearing the siren, took shelter under the stairs. Within a few minutes bombs fell on both sides of the vicarage wrenching off three heavy doors and damaging the kitchen near where the Vicar was sheltering. The Vicar's dog found refuge in the only room in the house that was untouched by the blast. A canary in its cage in the dining room was also unhurt.

Chapter 2, 1940

There was a train at a standstill nearby, at the time of the raid, and many of its windows were blown out by the blast of exploding bombs. A number of passengers in this train suffered injuries by flying glass.

One of the Heinkel bombers flying south, turned over Seaham to head out to sea, glycol smoke streaming from one engine that had stopped. The other engine was surging and not maintaining enough power to keep the aircraft airborne. As it crossed the shore its bombs were jettisoned into the sea, exploding with a deafening noise. Three Hurricanes pounced on this luckless, crippled aircraft that came down into the sea. The plane rested on the surface for about five minutes before sinking below the waves. The lifeboat was launched and searched the area but there were no survivors. The crew were either dead or to badly injured to make their escape from the plane while it lay on the surface.

After the raid, children in Parkside came out of their shelters and began collecting shrapnel that had fallen in the streets. A small field, between Daphne Crescent and The Dene, had two unexploded bombs several feet into the earth. Air-raid wardens kept a small crowd of people

from getting to near while they waited for the bomb disposal group to arrive. Three fighters, returning to base, roared over Parkside and the small group of people cheered and waved to them. The last of the three fighters did a 'victory roll,' bringing more cheering. On returning to base this pilot was strongly admonished by his wing commander for performing the 'victory roll,' which might have damaged a valuable aircraft. However, that 'victory roll' was a great morale booster for the cheering crowed standing by the wooden railings. One of the houses in Daphne Crescent received hits from cannon fire thought to have been from the Heinkel but they were more probably fired by the chasing fighters.

During the raid a hen was about to lay an egg when a bomb dropped close by destroying the hen house and blowing the hen several yards away though it seemed unhurt by the experience. The egg was found still in the nest and in one piece.

On Saturday afternoon the Marquess and Marchioness of Londonderry accompanied by Malcolm Dillon, agent, and Mr P. Wilson, manager of Dawdon Colliery, paid a visit to Seaham to inspect the damage that had been done to houses in the raid. They also called upon the Reverend Duncan at the church and spoke to members of the public in Dawdon, sympathising with those who were bereaved and injured.

At a meeting on Monday 19 August, the Executive Committee of the Durham Miners' Federation had a proposal before them to consider handing over £10,000 for the purpose of buying two Spitfires. The proposal, if accepted by the miners, was seen as the appropriate answer to Hitlers bombing attack over the North East coast. Will Lawther said that they would hand over to the R.A.F. two Spitfires that would harass still further these "murderers of the air."

Also on this day the funerals of those who had been killed in the attack took place. The Chairman of Seaham Urban Council, Mr H. F. Lee and the Clerk to the Council, Mr J. C.

Edington, attended. Each coffin carried a wreath from Lord and Lady Londonderry that was inscribed with the words, 'With deep sympathy from the Marquess and Marchioness of Londonderry.' The sad procession to Seaham Cemetery passed silent crowds where men stood bareheaded.

The first funeral was that of Mr Thomas Rochester (44) and his wife Eleanor (47) and also their daughters Eileen (19) and Joice (14). A detachment of the Home Guard attended as did officials of the Miners' Lodge. Mr Rochester had been a colliery deputy and also a member of the Home Guard. The Reverend James Duncan held the service.

A home service was conducted by the Reverend Duncan and the Reverend A. J. Cross at the funeral of Mrs Barbara Ferry (48) and her daughter Doreen (14). Rev. Duncan officiated at the graveside. Mrs Ferry had been a member of Seaham Townswomens' Guild, Doreen was a member of the Girl Guides and both organizations sent wreaths. A small detachment of Girl Guides also attended the service.

Mrs Edna Tempest (30) was the next cortege to follow mourned by her husband, Mr Charles Tempest, wearing his naval uniform, brother in the navy and two brothers-in-law in the army, also attended. The Reverend E. N. O. Gray held the service in the church and at the graveside.

The funeral of Mrs Sarah Shaw (55) and Daughter Mrs Mary Johnson (29) followed with a service at the home and at the cemetery conducted by the Reverend Duncan. Mrs Shaw was a widow from the First World War and her daughter was employed at Seaham Hall Sanatorium. Mrs Johnson's husband, a miner, was the chief mourner and representatives of the Miners' Lodge were present, as were nurses from the sanatorium.

The last funeral was that of Mr Edward Swan (36) who was a colliery banksman. Miners' Lodge representatives were Mr R. Lawson and Mr W. Thompson and the service was conducted by the Reverend E. N. O. Gray.

The people of Seaham had now come face to face with the realities of the air war and, though shaken, got on with their lives with the determination to see it through to the end. There would be other air-raids on Seaham, the people knew that but mining communities were no strangers to living with danger and perhaps they were better prepared for any future terror than many other communities in the country.

On Wednesday 21 August, the Broxon brothers of Murton had something to celebrate. A racing pigeon that they owned and which they had sent to Holland in July 1939, returned to their loft. Many times they had tried to have the bird returned to them but without success. The little red and white bird now in occupied Holland had been away from home for a year before being finally released. One of the brothers said at the time, "It is now the pride of the loft and would not be a Hitler bird."

At a meeting this week of New Seaham Working Mens' Club, it was decided to lend to the Government £1,000 free of interest until the end of the war. This gesture was typical of the spirit among local groups that every means should be looked at to see if there could be some way to help the war effort.

This spirit was not confined to the adult population alone but children too made the effort to raise money. Over the weekend of 24 and 25 August, thirteen children who had been evacuated for two days, decided it was time to do something themselves to defeat the enemy. Led by the two older girls, Marion Fail (13) of Ranksborough Street and Tessie Lennox (14) of Stanley Street North, who organised things, the other younger children began their campaign. This younger group included, Rita Fail (5), Edna Lennox (12), Joe Lennox (3), Hazel Oliver (8), June Sandy (6), Betty Pemberton (9), Theresa Scholin (11), Margaret Cowan (9), Vera Watson (8), Frances Watson (10) and Hazel Bell (10). This little group raised the sum of £1 6s 7d and sent the donation to Mr F.H. Lee, Chairman of Seaham Urban Council, for the 'Spitfire Fund.' Mr Lee forwarded the money to the Sunderland 'Spitfire Fund' as Seaham did not have a 'Spitfire Fund' of its own at that time.

Another fund-raising appeal was made to the parishioners of Dalton-le-Dale by the Chairman of the Parish Council, Mr Henry Crow. Donations to the fund would be in the form of a thanksgiving for their safe deliverance after the recent air-raids when bombs were dropped in all of the surrounding districts. "We owe our safety and survival to the vigilance of the Royal Air Force and the gunners of the Anti-aircraft Batteries, who are able to speak to the raiders in a language they understand," said Mr Crow.

A house-to-house collection among the 230 residents raised £28. This figure would have been larger but a number of residents had already sent their donations directly to the specific services. The £28 was handed over to the Mayor of Sunderland for the 'Spitfire Fund.'

The Bishop of Durham, Dr A T. P. Williams, visited Seaham on Wednesday 29 August, to inspect the damage that had been done to Dawdon Church and the Vicarage during the air-raid. He also visited a number of houses that had been damaged. Dr. Williams spoke to Mr Campbell whose daughter, Mrs Gale, had just died in hospital from injuries she received in the raid. He expressed his sympathy with Mr Campbell and other relatives.

Despite the threats of doom broadcast by 'Lord Haw Haw' on German radio William Skilbeck proudly announced the opening of new garage premises at Cliffe House Garage on Monday 2 September. Gestures of optimism for the future progress of business development in Seaham were being made in the face of mounting difficulties and the opening of Skilbeck's Garage was a welcome sign of such optimism.

Towards the end of September Lord and Lady Londonderry made a generous offer to the people of the East End of London who had suffered the loss of their homes through enemy bombing. As the Marquis and Marchioness spent much of their time in their beloved Mount Stewart home in the eastern shores of Northern Ireland, they decided to give their London home up to the shelter and hospitality of refugees from the East End. Those who had been blitzed from their homes were offered accommodation in Londonderry House, Park Lane, London. Unknown to Lord Londonderry at the time of the offer, a bomb had exploded close to Londonderry House and had blown out every window, however, work was soon put in hand to replace the windows and make the building habitable once more.

The loss of France brought great problems to the mineworkers of Durham as coal could not now be exported to France. Coal output had to be curtailed because of this new situation. The government suggested that miners could possibly be retrained and sent into other industries. Miners' representatives were sure that coal miners could adapt to other industrial skills but the Minister of Mines felt that it might be more useful to place men in other coal fields such as Staffordshire of Lancashire.

At the beginning of October, Dawdon Miners' Lodge received notice from the management that because of slackness in the coal trade one of the seams would have to close and shifts in the other parts of the mine would be reduced from three to two. This meant that about 700 men and boys would lose their jobs. The Miners' Lodge asked for time to work out a shift rota system so that all of the men might share the burden. Negotiations began with management without delay as it was felt that homes would be broken up if men were paid off.

Both sides met at the Londonderry Offices, Seaham, in a very friendly atmosphere. Each was aware of the serious effect if 700 men were put out of work and it was agreed that a rota system would work. The effect of the proposals was that the whole work force, over 2,000 men and boys, would work two weeks out of three. In the week when men would be off work, those living in colliery houses would pay rent and those in private rented housing would receive no rent allowance from the employer. Holiday credits for these weeks would also be suspended.

Air raids during the night were causing problems, mainly through disturbing sleep, when people were obliged to go to their shelters while bombers flew overhead on their way to other targets. Anti-aircraft fire was loud and furious and many mothers and children huddled together under the stairs for some hours until the 'all clear' siren sounded.

The Reverend C. R. Appleton made an inspiring farewell sermon on Sunday 20 October. He took as his text, 'Watch ye, stand fast in the faith, quit you like men, be strong.' (1 Cor. XVI., 13) In part of his address he showed how ordinary people could handle change. "Times of crises test us and prove what manner of people we are. Times of crisis make some people. In ordinary times they appear just very ordinary people but in times of crisis they rise to hights well above themselves. How often great and unexpected bravery has been exhibited by people during air raids when ordinary people have shown themselves to be more than heroes by acts of supreme courage." He spoke of how he hoped that those in the parish that he had been unable to influence would, perhaps, be influenced by the new incumbent, the Reverend O. N. Gwilliam.

In Murton on Sunday 1 November, there was a talk given in the Miners' Hall by Mr William Courenay, a London journalist and aviator. The talk was entitled, 'The progress of the Air War' and was organised by the East Durham Nucleus Committee of the Ministry of Information. The hall was full of local people who listened intently as Mr Courtenay explained the difference between the German outlook towards the aeroplane for military purposes and that of the British. The Germans had used and were using the bomber as an instrument of terror, to panic the civilian population to such an extent that they became refugees and pressed their governments to sue for peace, as we have seen in many countries in Europe.

"They tried that on here," said Mr Courtenay, "but it did not work. Our people were proof against panic and that made all the difference. A people like ours, who had built up a great Empire, a proud, sturdy, strong, independent people, were not going to panic."

The pattern of bombing that Britain was carrying out in Germany was a strategy against the weak point in the German armoury and that was its oil supplies. Germany had imported about five million tons of oil from America but since the war started the British Navy had largely shut that tap off. Germany had built about fifty hydrogenation plants producing about three million tons of oil from coal. It was the R.A.F.s first task to hit these plants hard and so far it was reported that 75% of hydrogenation plants had been knocked out. The next task was to attack the crude oil that Germany was receiving from Rumania. This was why the R.A.F. was visiting the port of Hamburg where the crude oil was going into the refineries.

Mr. Courenay also showed his audience how we were bombing German aircraft factories and munitions factories. His talk was presented in an optimistic and positive way and Coun. E.W. Toft thanked Mr Courtenay for his enlightening talk on behalf of the East Durham Nucleus Committee and the audience.

During the first week of November two young ladies held a jumble sale in a back yard. Miss Edwards and Miss Dickinson of Wynyard Street, Dawdon, raised £2 and sent the money immediately to the Lord Mayor of London's Air Raid Distress Fund.

Also this week comforts for sailors was on the minds of Betty Philips of Daphne Crescent and Joyce Foulds of Beech Crescent, Seaham when they held a jumble sale in a back yard. They raised 16s that were handed to Mr J. W. Swales, Missioner to Seaham Seamens' Mission.

Seaton branch of the W.V.S., which was only formed last August, had already sent parcels of woollen goods, sweets and cigarettes to the value of 5s each to 21 Seaton men serving in the forces. In addition, 52 pairs of socks and 16 woollen helmets had been sent to Seaton Home Guard members and socks, cigarettes and chocolate sent to a local Searchlight Battery. The hospital at Ryhope now treating many wounded service men had also been visited and chocolate, cigarettes and other gifts were left for the patients. The W.V.S. also raised £9 for the Spitfire fund.

At the Cosy Cinema, New Seaham, the Murton Womens' Institute Choir and Drama Group gave an entertainment to raise money for the Seaton Wool Comforts Fund. Besides songs and other items there was a play called, 'No 10.' The choir was conducted by Mrs Short. 'War Weapons Week' began on 2 November. This was a saving drive to finance the manufacture of much needed weapons.

A hand book was published in the first week in November by Seaham Council stating the rights, privileges and responsibilities of tenants in Council housing. The booklet pointed out that any damage to council houses had to be paid for through rent increases so it was in tenants interests to care for the property at all times. Good neighbourliness was also highlighted as a quality required in each tenant if the new estates were to be the best places to live. A three - bedroom cottage in Deneside had a rent of 10s 1d per week but only 5s 9d was in fact actual rent the rest was made up of 3s 6d general rate 10d water rate. The services provided through the 3s 6d general rate included education of children and their free examination by doctors and other health services. There were also libraries, roads and paths, sewage disposal, fire brigade and police.

The 5s 1d rent, it was pointed out, does not go in profit to the Council; the Council is not allowed by law to make a profit. Every penny not required for loan charges or maintenance must be passed back to the tenants by lowering rents. The Council was determined to put everyone in the picture and emphasised the need for good citizenship and community, long being the aspirations of the people of the town.

A memorial service was conducted for Mr Walter Robinson in the Seamens' Mission Church, Seaham, on Sunday 3 November. Mr Robinson lost his life on a Minesweeper. Mr W. J. Swales, Missioner, said in his address that the men of the Royal Navy and Mercantile Marine were giving of their best, even of life itself. "We thank God for their grand and glorious traditions and service. They must succeed because their cause was right," said Mr Swales.

'War Weapons Week' ended in Seaham and the people were praised for their efforts in contributing such a grand total. The Seaham Urban Area had raised £45,727-0-11d. Not counting the £10,000 contributed by the Urban Council and the £15,000 subscribed by the three local banks the public had still raised nearly £21,000 as individuals.

The week ended with a procession in Seaham led by Dawdon Band and included a military detachment, Home Guard, Civil Defence, Police, British Legion, Boy Scouts and Guides and other organisations. A model warship was displayed along with armoured cars and guns. There were a number of tableaux in the procession displaying the work of the W.V.S., the Townswomens' Guild, Red Cross and the Urban Council. Last of all came the tableau depicting Adolph Hitler on the gallows. This was presented by Mr Charlie Keegan, a well - known local comedian, and his party.

Coun.H. F. Lee said that Seaham did remarkably well over the week and he drew attention to the part played by schools where the sum of £500 had been donated. This amount must have meant considerable self denial by many families for such a good cause.

A concert was held at the Theatre Royal, Seaham on Sunday 17 November in aid of the Easington Spitfire Fund. Among those taking part were the well - known entertainers Mr Frank E. Franks and Gene Boyne with full supporting company. A large audience thoroughly enjoyed the afternoon.

Chapter 2, 1940

It was announced this month that the Government would introduce a scheme to aid unemployment among miners who were now out of work because of the loss of coal export markets to Europe. Mr. Sam Watson, Unemployment Officer at the Durham Miners' Association, outlined the idea of training in engineering to enter into war work in the engineering industry.

A fourteen page booklet was published to explain the scheme whereby unemployed miners and temporary unemployed miners could take advantage of this training. Trainees would be allowed to remain members of the Durham Miners' Association until they had finished training. If at that time they decided to go into war work then they would need to leave the Miners' Association and join the appropriate engineering union. There were seventeen Government Training Centres with 12,000 places so this was seen as a welcome initiative and for those who would take the challenge, a new and rewarding way of life.

Many donations were handed over to the Reverend James Duncan, Vicar of Dawdon Church, during the first week of December. The money came from all denominations to help with the restoration of the church that was badly damaged by the bombing on 15 August. One of the first donations came from Father M. J. Haggety, Dean of St. Mary Magdelene's Church; he and the vicar were, of course, good friends.

The level crossing at the north end of Princess Road was closed from midnight on Saturday 7 December until 5a.m Sunday in order that the N.L.E.R. could carry out maintenance work on the track. This was the busiest crossing in Seaham and traffic intending to reach Seaham Harbour during this closure was diverted to Dawdon or New Seaham. Though the New Road scheme was underway there was no sign of any progress of the proposed subway under the rail line that would eventually lead to the closure of the busy crossing.

Meetings of many kinds were held in Seaham and Murton and were very well attended. There was a great need for people to know what was going on in the area and how they could help. Information on any relevant subject was keenly sought and debated upon and on Friday 13 December Madame D'Alrey (in private life she was Mrs Marceline D'Alrey Besley, a London journalist) spoke on 'Women, War and Work.' The meeting was held in the Salvation Army Hall and was arranged by the East Durham Nucleus Committee of the Ministry of Information and was presided over by Mrs T. Todd.

In the Church Hall, Seaham Harbour, the St. John's Young Peoples' Fellowship was debating 'That things are Getting Better Every Day.' This motion was carried by a large attendance. Though this might seem a little optimistic in hindsight it perhaps shows that the spirit of the younger generation at least was not downcast.

Home nursing classes were started in the Camden Square School, one for men and one for women and the lecturer was Dr. Sacks. There were also classes in First Aid in connection with A.R.P. work. Similar classes were also held in the Seaham Intermediate School.

This week, Mr. John McCutcheon had an exhibition in Seaham Library of war photographs that had been provided by the Ministry of Information. These included photographs of enemy aircraft that had been brought down in this country and the Army and Navy at work, together with other relevant items. There was also a large piece of a German bomb that had been dropped at Dawdon on August 15 and also an incendiary bomb that had failed to ignite, also in the exhibition.

At Seaham Court a man from The Avenue, Deneside, was fined 40s for not obscuring his house light efficiently during the hours of darkness and a lady from Station Road was fined 20s for a similar offence. Usually any chink of light showing through blackout curtains would bring about loud banging on the window by an A.R.P. warden with a shout of "Put that light out."

While miners at Seaham and Murton were being made idle because of the loss of export markets some towns such as Manchester and others were reporting a coal shortage. There seems to have been slow reallocation of inland coal distribution after the loss of these export markets and it was felt that, if the Midland's Coalfield could not supply these towns, then the Durham Coalfield would.

The Harbour Master, Mr Thomas Nicholson, Secretary of the Seaham Branch of the Royal National Lifeboat Institution, received a letter from Lieut. Col. C. R. Satterthwaite thanking the officials for their work during the past year. He said that the enthusiasm of all concerned and the generosity of the general public was of tremendous importance to the Lifeboat Institute. Ten lifeboats had taken part in the evacuation of Dunkirk, one was lost and all of the others were damaged in some way. The Lifeboat Committee and the Ladies' Lifeboat Guild were commended for all their hard work.

The delay in the provision of school shelters was causing concern. Factors responsible for the delays were identified in a report by Durham County Education Architect, Mr Fred Willey, by the middle of November. The report said that only 69 of the 229 school shelters had been built and that the delay was largely the fault of departmental muddle. There were cases where trenches were dug to site the shelters but these had filled with water. This brought about delay while permission was sought to finance drainage. In Seaham three special shelters were urgently needed, these were of fabricated steel and the manufacturer only had three in stock. The Board of Education in Durham was told that the matter was urgent but the necessary licence was not issued until four or five weeks had elapsed. By this time the shelters had been sold to someone else.

The Medical Officer for Seaham, Dr J.R. Hetherington published his annual report in November and had a few hints for keeping healthy. He emphasised the importance of sleep especially for the young and that the best medicines were free, sunshine, fresh air, sleep and water. Dr. Hetherington stressed the need for cleanliness. "Where there is dirt there is danger. If you wish to remain healthy use plenty of water both inside and out both for yourself and your house." It was reported that births in Seaham in 1939 were 485 giving a rate of 16.3; there were deaths numbering 300 a rate of 10.6 and infant mortality stood at 78 per thousand live births.

In the first week of December a number of miners who had applied to leave the local coal mines to train as aircraft fitters, left for training centres in other parts of the country. Among the miners from Dawdon Colliery were Mr Bill Whitwell, Mr Jack Alexander and Mr Jack Potts. They trained at the Leeds Training Centre and, after qualifying, went on to aircraft production. Mr Whitwell worked at the A.V. Roe factory, Leeds involved in the production of Avro Anson and Lancaster aircraft while Mr Alexander was posted to a factory in Coventry where he worked on the production of Wellington bombers.

Seaham War Services Committee was sending out Christmas presents now in the form of 3s postal orders and knitted gifts to 1,300 service personnel from Seaham. Women members were busy at the beginning of December packing parcels and would be sending them off on Saturday 14th. Each parcel also contained a Christmas card from the donor. Over fifteen hundred woollen articles had so far been knitted by women members.

With just over a week to Christmas children in the area were enjoying Christmas parties as usual. On Saturday 14 December the Dalton-le Dale and Cold Heseldon Womens' Institute gave a Christmas party to 150 children. The children took part in games and received sweets and toys from Father Christmas (Mrs M. Laws). Entertainment was given by the children themselves.

Seaton W.V.S. raised £18 13s 6d from a sale of work in aid of Soldiers' Comforts Fund. Other fund-raising was going on at Deneside where Mr James Allen, of Ivy Avenue, and his friends held a number of whist drives and raised £20. The money was handed over to Mr J. Mortimer, Secretary of the Deneside Ward of the Seaham War Services Fund. There was also a small jumble sale organised by Misses Farrell and Ritchie of Bethune Avenue, Deneside and they did well to raise 7s for the same fund.

There was a new scheme underway in Seaham where the Council took to rearing pigs to supplement the food supply and it was paying its way. The collection of food scraps was producing ample amounts of pig food, housed on the old Chemical Works site near the Council salvage depot. This experiment in food production was started in August when a litter of seven small pigs of the 'Large-White' variety and only a few weeks old, was purchased. After four months they had attained a weight of 8 or 9 stones and were sold through the Pig Marketing Board at a local market.

After this sale a further 18 young pigs were bought and were being reared on the swill made from scraps collected during the normal runs of the Cleansing Department. This consisted of potato peelings, broken bread, scraps from the table, vegetable cuttings and other vegetable matter. All of this was boiled and mixed with 'boxings' and this work was done by young lads from the salvage work force one of whom had direct responsibility for the pigs as part of his duties.

Christmas time in Seaham was celebrated with all the enthusiasm that the situation would permit. Because of the stringent lighting restrictions Midnight Mass or Communions could not be conducted at either the Catholic or Anglican churches but celebrations on Christmas morning were all the more fully attended. A children's service was held later in the morning at Dawdon Parish Church followed by a sung Eucharist.

St. John's Church Choir visited Seaham Hall Sanatorium on Christmas Eve and sang carols. Many of the young women patients were moved to tears in the emotion of the evening. A member of staff, dressed as Father Christmas, distributed gifts to the patients on Christmas morning and later held a whist drive. At Hawthorn Tower a nativity Play arranged by Mrs K. Byrne and given by the children of Sunderland Nursery School, was a pleasant surprise for the rest of the staff and the children.

Ships in port were visited by Mr W. J. Swales, Missioner, and he invited seamen to the festivities at the Seamens' Mission Institute. There were a number of soldiers, who were away from home, also at the festivities. Christmas dinner consisted of roast turkey, goose and plum pudding and other seasonal fare and the guests later enjoyed a social evening.

The Seaham Lodge of the Durham Miners' Association submitted a resolution to the D.M.A. that, 'While we appreciate the endeavours of our agents and executive committee in looking after the interests of our members transferred to other counties, we are of the opinion that a concentrated effort should be made with a view to Durham coal being transported to other places thereby finding employment for those in our own county.' A statement by the D.M.A. underlined the miners' solidarity and hope for 1941 in the struggle against Fascism and their determination to assist in its overthrow was being drawn up and would be sent by wireless and dropped as leaflets to the miners of Europe.

Because of the situation at this time, the dock area was a prohibited area except for those who worked there. However, Seaham Council authorised the Clerk to enquire of the military authorities whether permission might be given for local fishermen to visit the docks for angling purposes. Fish was very scarce and it was felt that anything that could help to increase the supply would be a step in the right direction.

Recycling of valuable resources was going well and it was reported that in the last month of the year the Seaham Health Committee Salvage Department had dealt with 12 tons of flattened tins and 5 tons 11 cwt of waste paper.

The year had been a traumatic experience with the full realisation that things could get worse before they got better. Throughout the British Isles there came many changes; road signs were removed and railway stations had their names painted out so that in the event of an enemy invasion some confusion might ensue to hinder troop movements.

We had seen the introduction of food rationing in January of this year. Long queues in miners' halls waited for hours to collect new ration books and long queues at the Co-op, or wherever families had registered for their food rations, became normal life.

Winston Churchill became Prime Minister in May of this year. Although perceived as no friend of mining communities, indeed his appearance on British Movietone News at the Cosy Cinema would, in the early days, produce some booing, this was the beginning of Churchill's 'finest hour.'

The British housewife was asked in July to give aluminium pots and pans to aid aircraft production. A number of places in Seaham were set aside to receive aluminium items. In Murton these items were collected and sorted from scrap metal in a receiving point at the top of Woods Terrace.

Adolf Hitler issued a directive this month for the invasion of Britain. The Battle of Britain was about to begin and Seaham had a taste of daylight air warfare on 15 August. Many local men joined the Local Defence Volunteers (LVD) as invasion fears grew. The LDV (who were rather unkindly known as 'Look, Duck and Vanish') was renamed Home Guard but there was a desperate shortage of weapons. One group under the command of a first world war retired colonel who, alone, had a .22 rifle, ordered his men to gather large stones from the beach and place them on the cliff tops ready to throw down onto invading German troops. The 'Invasion Imminent' warning had gone out throughout the country and these true patriots in Seaham were ready to offer what resistance they could.

Chapter 3, 1941

The Tightening of Belts

The year began on a sombre note with the announcement that the meat ration was to be cut. The shortage of merchant ships through losses in the Atlantic meant that ships that had been used for the transportation of meat from Argentina were now being diverted to the Middle East carrying munitions to the 8th Army in Libya. Belts would have to be tightened yet again.

However, all was not doom and gloom by any means as the pantomime season was now underway. The Seaham Amateur Operatic Society staged one of the best shows in the last thirty two years of its existence. The show at the Theatre Royal was 'Babes in the Wood' and was believed to be the only amateur production being staged in the North this season. As usual the proceeds from the show were being given to local charities. Over the last three years these charities had received more than £300 from this group of dedicated Operatic Society members.

Because of an unfortunate illness Mr John Taylor, who was cast in the roll of the Sheriff of Nottingham, had to drop out of the production. Into the breach stepped Mr Fred Haydon a soldier from the South of England who was billeted near by. He did an excellent job at very short notice.

Robin Hood was played by Violet Oughtred and Mrs Belsie Morries played Maid Marion. The audience rocked with laughter at Miss Betty Davison's 'Dame Humbug' and her school. The theatre was in uproar as she lead the audience with a hilarious song called, 'Push the Damper In.'

'Dirty Dick' and 'Soapy Sam' were played by George Shepard and Jack Gentles. Billy Hardy had a lot of work in the character of 'Baron Butterscotch.' The 'Babes' were played by eight years old Jaqueline Gentles and eight years old Brian Elgy with great effect and brought much applause with their song, 'Give a Little Whistle.'

There were air-raid warnings most nights keeping the citizens of the town out of their beds for some hours. One Heinkel 111. was picked up by a search light battery that was stationed in a field on the south side of Grangetown Cemetery, at about 6p.m. on February 15. The Heinkel was hit by anti-aircraft fire and was thought to have struck a barrage balloon cable before crashing at Bents Park, South Shields. One of the crew, Oberfeldwebel Wilhelm Beetz managed to bail out but was killed when he collided with trolley bus electric contact wires. Beetz was buried in Castletown Cemetery, Sunderland along with the rest of

Chapter 3, 1941

his crew, Gefreiter Franz Janeschitz, Unteroffizier Helmut Jeckstadt, and Unteroffizier Karl Brunzen. Hauptman H. Styra, the fifth crew member was not found and was declared 'Missing presumed dead.'

It is entirely possible that it was this aircraft that had dropped bombs on Seaham that night. Houses in Frederick Street, Seaham Harbour were hit and also the subway between Lord Street and Ropery Walk received a direct hit.

In the early hours of the next morning 16 February, at about 2.30 a.m. there were more raiders overhead. These had been attacking targets in Middlesbrough, Hartlepool, Seaham and Sunderland. In Seaham, houses in Stewart Street were hit and destroyed and 257 houses in the town sustained some damage. The night's action had claimed five lives with about a dozen people injured. Among the dead were Margaret Wilkinson aged 36, Paricia Wilkinson aged 4 years old and Norman Wilkinson who was just one year old.

A great snowstorm developed in February and snow fell continuously for forty hours beginning Tuesday 18th. Snow to a depth of more than two feet covered the county with drifts of six to eight feet. Road transport was at a standstill for at least three days and trains were held up for hours. Buses and cars were stranded in deep snow. Those people who did not work in Seaham and managed to get to their place of work, had to find lodgings until a skeleton bus service could get underway.

At local coal mines those working 'on bank' were sent out to cut tracks in the snow leading to the pit. Even then many men could not get through the deep snow to start their shift. Households were finding it hard going with severe shortages of bread, meat, milk and coal because all roads were impassable.

A new initiative was launched that would supplement the food ration. Because of the success of the pig rearing scheme run by Seaham Urban Council the rearing of table rabbits was suggested and this was approved by the council. The scheme would be in the form of a co-operative venture rather than a totally council project. The Parks and General Purposes Committee met on Tuesday 25 February and approved the idea. The Town Surveyor, Mr J. B. Abbey co-ordinated the project that aimed to provide quickly fresh and wholesome meat to augment the meat ration. A useful by-product of the venture was the fur that could be used to make mittens and hats for children.

Waste greens from allotments were to be used to feed the rabbits as well as greens from roadside verges. Pea pods were gathered and dried to be used as winters feed and would be soaked in water before being given to the stock. There was some spare ground for growing root vegetables for other winter feed.

The main stock comprised of Blue Beverin and Flemish Giant rabbits that produced quality meat as well as good quality fur. The husbandry of stock was on a voluntary basis but hutches were provided by the Council. Schools were asked to co-operate with the venture and some condemned houses were used to house some of the hutches. Throughout the summer months the plan was to house the rabbits in Morrant hutches that would allow the rabbits to feed on grassed areas and could be moved to new sites on waste land every few days. Four does and one buck would be introduced in each centre and rabbits would be ready for table from three months old.

Mr Ernest Bevin M.P. spoke at a meeting in the Regal Cinema, Durham on Saturday morning 10 March. In answer to one question he said that he believed that the coal industry would become publicly owned after the war.

The Vestry Committee and Parochial Committee met on Tuesday evening 1 April and the vicar, the Reverend S. Kearney spoke of how the people of the town should be proud to live in this area in our history and proud of the cause that had brought so much unity to the country.

The debate on the playing of sport on Sundays was continuing and the Rector of West Rainton, the Reverend C. S. Nye, said he did not approve of cinemas opening on Sunday but thought that some games such as tennis, bowls and golf were soul refreshing and a good thing provided they did not interfere with the hours of worship.

A well-known Seaham sportsman, Mr. E. Whitelock, Secretary of Seaham Harbour Cricket Club said he had no time for organised sport on Sundays though individual sport such as swimming were acceptable. Organised sport meant that teams would have to travel along with their supporters and that meant that someone would have to work on a day which they might want as a day of rest.

Throughout April air-raids at night continued and the spirit of everyone in the town showed itself when it was learned that boy messengers 'fought with each other' for the right to carry messenger to civil defence units in the town even when bombs were falling.

A well-liked teacher and Headmaster Mr T. E. Venner, a native of New Seaham, was interred at Christ Church on Saturday 19 April. Mr Venner was Headmaster of Belmont Church of England School and also a well-known Free Mason.

The Ministry of Aircraft Production, Lord Beaverbrook, sent a bronze plaque on an oak base to be presented to the Durham Miners' Association with the inscription, 'In the hour of peril the Durham Miners' Association earned the gratitude of the British Nation sustaining the valour of the Royal Air Force and fortifying the cause of freedom by the gift of two Spitfire aircraft, 'They shall mount up with wings.'

The Scout Movement conferred a great honour on one of Seaham's best known member of the community on Sunday morning 27 April. Mr. Malcolm Dillon was presented with the 'Silver Acorn' by Lord Barnard, County Commissioner and the decoration was the second highest honour in the scouting movement. The 'Silver Acorn' was awarded by Chief Scout, Lord Somers, for Mr. Dillon's long and valued service.

The presentation was carried out at a combined parade of Boy Scouts and Girl Guides outside St. John's Parish Church at the end of a parade service in the church conducted by the Reverend O.

Chapter 3, 1941

N. Gwilliam who said that the Scout and Guide movement stood for all that is chivalrous, upright and noble and that an honour such as this meant that when one member of a body receives such an honour the whole body is honoured. The ceremony ended with a march past by Scouts and Guides with Lord Barnard taking the salute.

Production of the new Morrison shelter was now underway but as they were as yet in short supply there was a list of towns drawn up which would receive the first off the production line. Newcastle was the only town in the Northern Region on this list. With increasing production it was hoped that deliveries would be quickly widened.

The Morrison shelter was designed to be constructed indoors and was made of steel in the form of a large table. The base was crossed with a lattice of sprung steel strips on which a mattress could be laid. The flat top was made of a quarter inch sheet of steel and would protect the occupants from tons of falling brick rubble. The shelter could be and was used in most cases as a table. During air-raids the owner would place the steel wire mesh around the sides and clip them into position from the inside. They became wonderful dens for children to play in on rainy days and the underside of the table made a great blackboard to chalk on. Of course many of the drawings in chalk depicted aircraft dropping bombs, tanks and guns being fired. Morrison shelters were available free to anyone with an income of less than £350 P.A. If the income was more than that then the shelter could be bought for £7.

A Messerschmitt fighter aircraft with drop tanks fitted, crossed the North Sea on Saturday night 10 May. It was piloted by the Third Nazi Chief of the Reich the Party Leader Rudolf Hess. He bailed out over Scotland leaving his aircraft to crash. He was trying to contact the Duke of Hamilton whom he had met before the war at a sporting meeting. He hoped to find a way to end the conflict. The Nazis said that Hess was suffering from a mental disturbance.

Posters were put on display in Seaham and the rest of the county by the Durham Miners' Association and the Mine Owners asking the miners to 'Put their backs into it.' This was a drive for the production of yet more coal to fire the nation's war effort. However, not everyone accepted this without question. Some voiced the opinion that when the miner was needed to produce more coal he was looked upon as a saviour of his country but that no one cared when the mines went on short time and the men were only able to work two weeks out of every three. This gave the miner a take home pay of £2 5s 6d for two weeks work and only thirty shillings for the next.

A new rationing order was issued by the Government on Sunday morning 1 June. The Clothes Rationing Order that was introduced meant that clothes and footwear were now only available on production of the required number of coupons.

A surprise visitor arrived in Murton on Saturday 21 June when Canadian soldier Pte. Tim Sheedy knocked on the door of Mrs J. B. Short, President of Murton Women's Institute. Some time ago the Institute had contacted a village Institute in Canada suggesting that the Murton organisation would like to 'adopt' a Canadian soldier. Tim Sheedy who was already in England with the Canadian forces was selected. A further surprise for the Murton organisation was that Tim had brought his new bride, Mary, with him. He had met Mary, an English girl, eighteen months earlier and they had been married when Tim had leave.

The couple spent their week visiting other members of the Women's Institute and at a party on Saturday 28 Mrs Short presented a wedding present to the couple on behalf of the Institute. The couple said they felt very lucky to have been adopted by such kindly people.

[Authors Note: In 1998 I used the Internet to try to trace Tim or his family. The first Tim Sheedy I found was not the man as he was born long after the war but he was able to put me in touch with Ken Sheedy who was the Sheedy family historian. Ken soon realised that the man I was looking for was his older brother. The next e-mail from Ken told me I was in luck as Tim had aquired a computer and was now on-line. Tim, now eighty years old, remembers well the wonderful time he and Mary had among the folk of Murton. He remembers at the party held in their honour a piper playing them into the assembly and the wedding gift of a fireside companion set which is still proudly on display in his home. Unfortunately, Mary died in 1996 and the couple had never returned to England.]

In the Miners' Hall, Durham on Saturday 5 July miner's representatives in Durham County including those from Seaham heard an appeal by Admiral Sir Edward Evans (Evans of the Broke and of Antarctic fame) who came to urge the miners in the Durham coalfield to give the fullest effort in coal production over the next few months. He said that he was confident that the men would do everything possible to meet that request.

As if to underline that message, Sir Edward introduced the two pilots who were now flying sorties against enemy bombers and attacking ground targets in France with the two Spitfires that had been bought with £10,000 donated by the Durham Miner's Federation. They were welcomed with loud cheering.

The Minister for Aircraft Production had named the Spitfires 'Miners of Durham I' R.A.F. No. P8089 and 'Miners of Durham II' R.A.F. No. P8091. 'Miners of Durham I' was at that time flying with 43 Air Fighting Development Unit and 'Miners of Durham II' was with 74 Squadron. This squadron was stationed at R.A.F. Gravesend during May and arrived for service at its new base at R.A.F. Acklington, Northumberland on 9 July.

The two pilots were Flight Lieutenant J. N. McKenzie D.F.C. New Zealand and grandson of the former New Zealand Prime Minister, Sir Thomas MacKenzie and Pilot Officer Balbage D.F.M. Flt. Lieut. Makenzie had 9 enemy aircraft to his credit and P.O. Balbage 8. P.O. Balbage said, "You have contributed two grand little aircraft. It would do your hearts good to see the number of Spitfires now flying over the other side on these sweeps. What these aircraft are doing now will seem only a trifle to what they will do when they are in full swing."

Sir Edward had brought a message from Lord Woolton, Minister of Food, who said, "I will do all that it is possible to do with the food resources at my command to see that the miners of the county are properly fed. All ready in many places pit-head canteens have been established. I hope that will rapidly increase in numbers and in usefulness. I will see that the necessary food is provided for them. Meanwhile, I am attaching to you (Sir Edward) a catering expert to press forward this development and to report directly to me."

There was a meeting in the Miners' Hall, Seaham Colliery, on Sunday morning 10 August. The main speaker was the M.P. for Seaham Mr Emanuel Shinwell. He told his audience that he believed the Prime Minister Mr Churchill was taking to much on himself. "He seems to be Prime Minister and everything else," he said. He told his audience that Mr Churchill should be prepared to co-operate with others by delegating work to colleagues and trusting in their abilities otherwise his administration would become a dictatorship. Churchill was resentful of any criticism which rather puzzled Shinwell as he was aware that in the past, Churchill had been critical of the Baldwin and Chamberlain Governments, the miners during the 1926 strike and even the people of India for daring to ask for Independence.

Mr Shinwell went on to say that right at the beginning of the war the coal industry should have been under direct State control with the administration in the hands of those who knew the industry. He doubted whether there would have been any coal shortage if this had been the case.

There had been a suggestion that there should be a guaranteed weekly wage for miners and Mr Shinwell had proposed this a year ago. Though he had been ridiculed about this suggestion at the time the very people who were originally against the idea were now claiming credit for its adoption. Wages in the industry were still poor even though the miners were being asked to give their all to coal production and in many ways they were even worse off. Miners were not allowed to go on strike and were under the threat of the severest penalties if they did. Local mine management also had more power over their workers than before the war started. Another sore point was the rate of pay being paid to munitions worker whose pay was much more enhanced than that of the miners.

This week a new parish priest was introduced to the town. Father Edward Avery was taking over the work of the late Dean Haggerty at St. Mary Magdalen's R.C. Church.

A trade union leader in Durham, under the pseudonym, 'Scraper Loader', issued a statement about the selection of M.P.s. He described himself as one who knows the Seaham Division intimately and that he felt that Mr Shinwell did not represent the views of the miners in his constituency. The question he posed was, 'Why did Seaham not have a miner as its M.P.?' He listed a number of people that he thought would be a credit to division, Joe Blackwell of Vain Tempest and W. Murphy of Murton, etc., were people that were well trusted and would make first class M.P.s from the miners own ranks.

An interesting sight was often to be seen around Seaham at this time. Albert Richardson could often be seen walking his pet fox on a lead as one would walk a dog. He had been working at a quarry near Boldon when a fox lair had been disturbed. The female fox fled with her litter but somehow one cub got left behind. Mr Richardson took the young fox, now called 'Tip,' home to the delight of his children aged one to six. The family also had a pet fox terrier and Mr Richardson also bred rabbits but all the animals lived peaceably together.

The First Lord of the Admiralty, A. V. Alexander was at a meeting in the Miner's Hall, Durham, on Saturday 30 August. He had come to the Delegate Conference arranged by the Durham Miners' Association to tell of the tremendous work the Royal Navy was doing in the fight to overcome Nazism. Although the conference was arranged by the Association there were many others there not connected with the coal industry who were equally keen to hear at first hand how the Senior Service was living up to its great reputation.

Mr Alexander praised the people of the North East for the help and assistance they had been to the Royal Navy. Ships had been built in record time both for the Navy and the Merchant Service on the Tyne, Wear and the Tees. There was also reconstruction and repair work going on as well as the conversion of ships to war purposes and running repairs.

The help given to Naval Officers by Mr J. J. Lawson M.P. Northern Deputy Commissioner for Civil Defence was much appreciated. Mr. Alexander continued, "I had been in office only a few weeks when I was faced with the task of how to get the British Army out of France following the defection of the French. That was the greatest task the Navy has ever faced, and indeed there is not a finer page in British Naval history than that series of day-by-day operations over three weeks, from the coasts of Holland, Le Havre, Cherborg, Brest and elsewhere during which we took nearly 600,000 souls out of France."

The enemy now had 2,000 miles of coastline under their control and we had 70 destroyers in dock undergoing repairs suffered during the evacuation at Dunkirk. There was the threat of invasion now that we had no troops left in France. The Navy had to counter attacks from surface raiders, air and submarine attacks and mines. The number of air attacks on ships was now so great because the enemy controlled all the air bases along the European coastline. Merchant ships had had their anti-aircraft defences doubled or trebled and many carried military gun crews. This latter was not allowed by international convention so some military gun crews dressed as merchant seamen.

Mr Alexander went on to outline his plans to introduce boys to the service through scholarship and going on through training to officer rank. The meeting was unanimous in reaffirming the loyalty of the Durham miners to the policies of the Labour Party and the Trade Union Congress in their fight against Nazi aggression and the preservation of liberty, freedom and the democratic institutions that were fundamental to world peace.

There was an air-raid over Seaham on Sunday 7 September and a policeman on patrol near the colliery yard saw a man strike a match to light a cigarette. Other workers in the yard were concerned that this action might be seen from the aircraft overhead. At the time bombs were already falling on the town. The 48 year old man was charged and later appeared in Court; he pleaded guilty and was fined £1.

After the Summer Savings Drive the National Savings Committee announced that there would be a campaign starting on October 18 and ending on March, 28, 1942 in which towns throughout the country would be asked to set aside one week in which to raise a sum that would represent the cost of building a warship. This week would be known as 'Warship Week' and the idea was to raise money to 'buy' a warship, whether it was one of the smallest vessels or a battleship.

It was envisaged that when each ship was commissioned that a replica plaque of the ship's badge would be presented to the town hall by the Admiralty together with a history of the ship's name. In turn a plaque would be placed on the quarter deck of the ship to commemorate the ties between the ship and the town.

Over the period of this campaign it was hoped that there would be friendly rivalry between different areas in order to create a greater amount of enthusiasm. The campaign was not intended to replace the group savings drive which would continue in parallel as that was also vitally important.

The Urban Council met on Tuesday night 23 September to adopt the General Rate that this time showed a drop of 11p in the pound for the half year ending in September 1942 compared with the rate ending in September 1941. Durham County's share of the rate was 6s 11/2p in the pound. Durham and Easington Assessment Committee took 1/4d and Seaham Urban Council and Burial Board required 2s 2 3/4d. Mr S. Barratt, Chairman of the Finance Committee moved the adoption of the estimates and said that the Committee had given nearly the whole of the reduction back to the people of the district.

It was also agreed to contact other urban councils for support in sending a protest to the Government about its attitude towards war damage insurance of council houses. Mr. Barratt said that of those houses which were scheduled to be demolished before the war and because of the war, were not, and these houses were included in the scheme then the annual liability of the Council would be between £3,000 and £4,000. However, if these houses were to be excluded then the liability would amount to about £3,000. The Council had been led to believe that the Government would be prepared to advance 75% of the money but now they had been told that councils would have to cover the cost themselves though the Government would consider applications for loans.

The Health Committee minutes showed the amount of salvage saved throughout the month of July. Waste paper - 6Tons 9cwt 1qr, Tins - 9Tons 4cwt, Bottles - 8cwt, Light Scrap Iron - 3Tons 9cwt, Aluminium - 1cwt 1qr. Income received from the sale of salvage from April to August amounted to £405. Also at this time there were 32 pigs in stock mainly fed on swill made from food scraps collected in the district.

There was some exciting news for the children of Seaham at the beginning of November. Durham County War Agricultural Committee had made representation to the County Education Committee to ask if school children could be given time off to help with the potato harvest. Because of the shortage of labour through men being away in the services or the munition factories the potato harvest was in danger of being left in the ground to rot. There were about 5,000 acres of potatoes yet to be harvested.

The Education Committee made the decision to close all elementary schools for one week beginning 6 November from east of a line from Consett to Wolsingham. The schools remained open to pupils under 12 years old and also for any children over 12 who wished to continue with their education. Farmers in the area were grateful for the help as children turned up in the early mornings to sign on with farmers such as Bulmer, Lawson, Weightman, Glaister around Seaham and Cutler, Lamb, Foster and Bell in the Murton area. Cold hands were warmed with mugs of tea and aching backs rested during short breaks while older women workers encouraged the youngsters to work hard.

Retailers in Seaham and Murton were coming in for some criticism when they displayed notices in their shop windows that were seen as discriminatory. Such notices as, 'DO NOT ASK FOR CIGARETTES, CHOCOLATE, ETC., UNLESS YOU ARE A REGULAR CUSTOMER.' 'CUSTOMERS SERVED FIRST' and 'NO CHOCOLATES ETC.', were irritating people who wanted to be able to buy such goods at any shop. It was suggested that some time in the future, when these shopkeepers were seeking trade, their attitude at this time would be remembered.

Mr F. L. Armstrong of Maureen Terrace, Seaham, a well known producer of local amateur drama, was underlining comments made by Miss Jeanne de Casalis the actress and radio broadcaster who had been speaking in the area about the threat to the theatre by local cinemas. He said that many small towns such as Seaham did not have the opportunity for professional repertory companies and the towns rely on the hard work of local amateur groups. This background was seen as the finest training ground for the budding actor and much better than the 'star' system that often subordinates everything else to the glorification of 'the star.'

By the middle of November the bulk of the potato harvest had been gathered in. Giving thanks to the school boys and girls for all their hard work, Mr J. W. Cassels, Executive Officer of the County War Agricultural Committee said, "But for their help it would have been really difficult to get the harvest in."

Also in November the Government issued a list of reasons for saving paper:

6 old books	-	will make 1 Mortar shell carrier
1 old book	-	will make 4 shell fuses
1 envelope	-	will make 1 cartridge wad
1 newspaper	-	will make 3 - 25lb shell cups

A happy event took place on Saturday 13 December with the wedding between Ralph Knox Millar, Second Officer Merchant Navy of Hawthorn Square and Miss Caroline Violet Boad of Longnewton Street, Dawdon. The bridegroom was one of the fortunate men who were rescued from the German prison ship Altmark.

Air-raids continued most nights with warnings sounding up to three times throughout the night. There were also the occasional daylight raids around the area. On Tuesday, December 9 a Long Range Reconnaissance Junkers 88 from 3(f)122 (F6+CL) was making to return to base in Eindhoven in occupied Holland. On its tail were two Hurricane fighters from Acklington in Northumberland. As the bomber crossed over Seaham children in shelters at Seaham High Colliery School were being encouraged to 'sing up' with their shelter songs such as 'Roll out the Barrel,' 'Run Rabbit Run,' which would help to drown out the noise of gunfire. Very soon a teacher swung open the steel door of the shelter and told the children they could come out - quickly. The children scrambled on to the top of the shelter to see the aircraft making out to sea with glycol smoke streaming. Slowly it sank towards the water and with a splash of spray, was gone.

Framed certificates from the Carnegie Trust Fund and a cheque for £10 each were awarded for 'heroic endeavour to save human life' to five Murton miners on Saturday night 20 December at the Rex Theatre by Mr George Raw, Agent and a director of the South Hetton Coal Company. The five men were John Skinner (49) Watkin Crescent, Henry Skinner (35) Grey Avenue, Joseph Wilson (30) Model Street, John Hanaby (32) South Coronation Street and John Gilbert (32) Brooklin Street. The award was in recognition of their bravery on April 2 last when a fall of stone in the five-quarter seam buried Mr John Abbot and trapping Mr Isaac Lowerson at the coal face. The five men set about a rescue operation immediately and after clearing about nine feet of the fall they found Mr Abbot but he was already dead. Large overhanging stone was likely to come down on the rescuers at any time so a decision was made to channel a way through to Mr Lowerson along the side of the fall. Clearing out a tunnel for a distance of 42ft with further falls of stone still occurring, the heroes reached Mr Lowerson in seven and a half hours and found him to be alive and unharmed.

Mr Raw went on to say, "We are here to honour five brave men. We are told by psychologists that the instinct of fear was a warning of danger and part of our instinct is self-preservation but the brave man was the one who knew the danger and suppressed the fear associated with it. I was thrilled in just hearing again the details of this rescue."

The last stanza of the poem, 'Miners', by Wilfred Owen perhaps sums up succinctly what many miners would think then and at the present time.

> And men will lull their dreaming lids
> While songs are crooned,
> But they will not think of us poor lads
> Lost in the ground.

A member of the public wrote to Seaham Urban District Council complaining about profiteering in the town. This letter was read out to Seaham Food Control Committee at a meeting on Monday evening 29 December. The letter stated that the writer had been charged 1s 9d at a local hotel for a glass of whiskey. The measure used was what was called a 'Lloyd George.' In addition, the same hotel charged 2s 2d for a small bottle of whiskey that held about a glass. Cider was being charged at 2s 2d when it was only recently 1s 2d and a bottle of lemonade was costing 8d which included a 1d on the return of the bottle.

The letter went on to point out that many people like to have a drop of spirit in the house for use during air-raids and was it not criminal that people should be so grossly overcharged. After discussion it was agreed the matter should be referred to the Regional

Food Office. Another complaint came from a woman who said that she lived quite a way from the nearest shop and when she saw oranges being taken into the shop she went in and asked to buy one. She was told by the shop assistant that she was not allowed to sell them until her boss returned to the shop. When the woman returned to the shop later the oranges had all been sold.

Mr S. Barratt, Chairman of the Committee said that he felt that it would be better if customers got their oranges at the shop where they got their rations. If retailers got their allocation of oranges in accordance with their rationed customers then people would get them normally but if they had to fight for them there would always be trouble.

Mr Shinwell M.P. at this time brought up the question of extra petrol for people who gave lifts to members of the services going on leave. However, Mr J. J. Llewellyn for the Ministry of War Transport said there was insufficient justification for extra petrol during the hours when public transport was running. Steps were being taken to economise transport so that extra public transport services could be introduced.

It was announced that Seaham would hold its 'Warship Week' from 7 to 14 February 1942 and interest in the event was being received with alacrity throughout the district. The Executive of the Seaham War Savings Committee met under the Chairmanship of Mr H. F. Lee and the guidance of Mr J. C. Edington, Clerk to Seaham Council.

A number of subcommittees were appointed to oversee the various aspects of the project. Throughout there were 120 savings groups in existence and the aim was to intensify the effort over the week that had been set aside for the purpose. Entertainment and other functions were arranged to make the week enjoyable and memorable. The Committee were hoping that the people of the town would support the savings drive and reach a target that would be worthy of the area. The Admiralty had already named a Minesweeper 'H. M. S. Seaham' at the launching ceremony in Renfrew on the Clyde. A sum of £65,000 was expected to be raised if the town was going to have the honour of adopting the Minesweeper and her crew.

Lord Londonderry was approached because of his direct interests in the town and Londonderry Collieries Ltd. so that a good start to the week would be made and so encourage people in the Seaham area to make the project a great success and reach the target that had been set. Mr Lee said, "We are therefore urging all citizens in the Seaham area to prepare themselves for a great campaign in the New Year in order to make this 'Warship Week' a colossal success. It is only a matter of six weeks before we will be in the middle of the biggest financial venture Seaham has ever tackled."

The savings habit had been growing for well over a year with Seaham joining in savings drives with other areas such as Sunderland and Boldon for War Weapons Week. This time Seaham would be counted on its own and a public meeting was to be held in the New Year to point out to people exactly what was expected of them. Every part of the town and every individual would be approached with a view to making the total figure the largest possible.

Chapter 3, 1941

It had been an anxious year with many nights disturbed by air-raids and, with many of the areas young men and young women away such as Peggy Stewart working in the Midlands making Boffars guns and Doris Wilson a Leading Aircraftswoman in the Women's Auxiliary Airforce, family life was very strange and many parents worried for the safety of their loved ones. Keeping things at home as normal as possible was the aim of most women in the North East.

Food supplies were low though everyone had their ration, as small as it was. There was some disgust when it was found that any retailer was deliberately holding back goods 'under the counter' for regular customers. There were cases of black market dealings for those who could afford to pay more but in general most people got on with things as best they could.

Christmas came and the season was celebrated much as usual considering the restrictions that were imposed. Carol services did take place in all the local churches and many servicemen were able to send Christmas greetings cards home from abroad on special micro filmed paper. Children had less to wake up to on Christmas morning though they did have books and board games such as 'Air-sea Rescue' that featured a shot down pilot in his rubber dingy moving across the board, with hopes of rescue raised or dashed with the throw of the dice. Life itself was much the same gamble.

Chapter 4, 1942

Holding Our Own

There were no church bells, colliery buzzers or hooters from ships in Seaham dock to greet the New Year of 1942 as there had been in years before the war. However, many people turned out 'first footing' to friends and relatives houses and wishing those they passed in blacked out streets, "All the best."

Because of the lighting restrictions it was difficult for churches to hold Watch Night Services though St. John's Parish Church had been blacked-out by this time so a Watch Night Service was conducted by the Reverend O. N. Gwilliam and when the New Year had been welcomed in the celebration of Holy Communion took place. Prayers were offered in conjunction with the Day of Prayer that was being observed in both Britain and America.

There was a concert in Murton Miners' Hall on New Years night given by Dalton-le-Dale, Cold Hesledon and Hawthorn village W.I. members. Guest artists included T. Rundle, T. Curtis, W. Ward and H. Wills. Songs, dances and sketches were performed collectively by Misses O. Coates, R. Vout, R. Colledge, Maughan Lowes, Bacon, McKillup, Laws, Ellison. B. Wilson was the accompanist. A model of H.M.S. Hawthorn that had been made by Mr Purvis of Murton was on display. All the proceeds from the show were to be given towards the 'Warship Week' effort.

A 'Dig for Victory' week had been called for but the New Year's frozen ground prevented any real participation. Attention was drawn to the need to produce more of our own food wherever possible. The campaign was set up to stimulate a greater interest in the vital movement for home food production.

Also this week a letter was set by the Durham Miners' Association to General Auchinleck commanding the 8th Army in North Africa. The letter congratulated him and the 8th Army for their success in Lybia. Mr Will Lawther has received acknowledgement from the Minister for War, Capt. Margeson, who said, "I'm sure that he and the troops, especially your own men in the D.L.I., will welcome this message."

The hard ground did not stop football matches taking place and on Saturday 17 Sunderland Reserves trounced Seaham St. Mary's by 10 goals to 1. Dawdon Colliery Welfare beat Seaham R.A. 3 goals to 2.

Morrison shelters were being distributed throughout Seaham. In some areas the high

Chapter 4, 1942

clay water table meant that outdoor Anderson shelters were unsuitable because of flooding after heavy rain.

A New Zealand Air Force Officer, Flight Lieutenant R. H. Laud married local girl Miss Doris Wilson in St. John's Church, Seaham on Saturday 17. Miss Wilson was the Leading Aircraftswoman in the Women's Auxiliary Air Force mentioned earlier.

Emanuel Shinwell spoke at a meeting convened by Seaham Divisional Labour Party and held in the Empire Theatre, Murton on Saturday. Shinwell went straight into the attack on those responsible for policy making. He said that the real enemies of the country were politicians who had failed to realise that we were up against the toughest proposition this country had ever had to face and those same politicians imagined that great orations, red tape and 'old school tie' methods were sufficient.

He felt that though the Prime Minister might be comforted by the support of his front bench and that of his back benchers it would not bring us any nearer to victory. He called for guarantees that all of the Government policies would be revised and that our productive capacity be fully utilised and that all 'bottle necks' and vested interests be removed. "This war is going to last a long time," he said, "and we have now an opportunity to rectify the mistakes of the past and gaining by experience."

This had been his theme throughout 1941 when he constantly criticised the Government not to seek its downfall but an overhaul of its production policies. He had said that the Government was like a ship that was carrying to much ballast. "Ballast may be useful, it keeps the ship steady. The trouble about the Government ship was that it was to steady. It seldom moves. In the words of the poet, Coleridge, 'A painted ship in a painted ocean.'" Ernest Bevin, Minister of Labour was not amused.

At this meeting there was also a motion carried unanimously deprecating the harsh prison sentences given to Kent miners who were protesting about wage rates. Shinwell said it was vindictive and a travesty of justice. " When black market racketeers offend against the law and destroy morale as well as lining their own pockets in an illegal fashion they are subjected to the moderate penalty of a fine and are free to pursue their nefarious activities once again. When miners who feel a natural resentment about their wages offend against the law they are sent to prison with hard labour," said Mr Shinwell.

At the beginning of February soap went on the 'ration'. There was a call for an additional quota for miners. Mr Will Lawther said that he felt that would not be a problem. In fact by the end of the month soap for miners was free from rationing.

A Seaham woman whose husband was a Flight Lieutenant in the R.A.F. before he was killed was told that from the first pay day in February her widows' pension would be £115 per year.

Because of the need for coal absenteeism in the mines was regarded as a civil offence and was counted by fining absentees a sum that was paid into Aged Miners' Homes Fund.

This was seen to be a more acceptable sanction than taking them to a Court of Law.

In March a start was made to remove all iron railings in areas of Seaham and Murton. The railings were needed to provide yet more iron for the making of shells and guns, etc. Also in March it was announced that there was to be a new 'National Mark' footwear. These very basic utility ware shoes would become available sometime in June.

Ministry of Transport Returns showed that 510 people were killed on the roads during February as compared to 689 for the corresponding month of 1941. There had been some improvement but deaths on the road were still very high and were largely due to the blackout.

A Dawdon airman with 100% disability was discharged from service with the R.A.F. and his pension was set at 29s 2d per week. On a lighter note, there was a happy occasion in Murton on Saturday 4 April when Gunner Fredrick Dodds married Miss Esther Bresnen. The couple were married in Holy Trinity Church and were attended by bride's maids Edith Armstrong and Rita Gray.

In Seaham this week the death was announced of Mr Joseph Elgy the Seaham timber merchant. Mr Elgy had been connected with the timber trade for 56 Years.

At the beginning of April there was a warning to children in Seaham schools not to touch or handle any strange objects that might be found lying in fields or derelict buildings. There was a chance that these were incendiary bombs, objects that look like Thermos flasks, metal balls or tubes with explosive charges inside. There had been children in other parts of the country who had been killed or injured and some who had carried live explosives home.

Sunday 5 April saw the introduction of compulsory queuing at bus and tram stops. Moving people from place to place was seen as better carried out in an orderly way particularly when workers needed to get to their place of work quickly.

By the end of the month the figure for the amount raised for 'Warship Week' was published. The total for the region came to an excellent £18.5 million but the news that the folk of Seaham were waiting for was that the town beat its initial target and had raised a staggering £101,691.

The 'Liberty Hair Cut' for women was all the rage now and the hairdressers in Seaham and Murton were busy with the new style. The hair cut was inspired by the regulations for women in the services and seemed to have caught on in a big way with women who were not in the services. A version of this hairdo was in vogue a few years earlier and was known as the 'semi-single' or 'Bingle.'

An ex-miner from Seaham Colliery who emigrated to Australia in 1926 and now at 35 years old was a Sapper in the Royal Australian Engineers wrote to his mother about life in the Middle East. Sapper George James Starling wrote to his mother, Mrs Starling of Parkside Crescent, Seaham saying he was well and the work he was doing kept him busy and kept his mined off 'other things.' He described how he had received his Tobruk Medal and in

Chapter 4, 1942

poems to his mother wrote about encounters with the enemy, one of which he called 'The Coves in Tobruk.' Another entitled, Kidding - In Memory of a Sapper,' reads:-

> When the Jerry bombs are fallin'
> From the flaming jaws of 'ell,
> And you'd give yer great possessions
> For a dinkum cosy dell;
> When ye 'iding, sweatin', fearin'
> In the nearest gapin' 'ole,
> Guess there's no time for kiddin'
> Yer just take it as yer dole.

Mr Douglas D. Murray was speaking, during the first week of May, on behalf of the majority of farmers in the area when he said that they were making great efforts to fulfil their patriotic duty to supply the countries needs. There was an impression taking hold that farmers were not following the general spirit of the people when it was learned that an airman, who had bailed out from a bomber after returning from a raid on Rostock, was charged 2d by a farmer in whose field he had landed when he asked to telephone his base in order to be picked up.

A combined exercise with the Home Guard and the Civil Defence took place over the weekend of 23 and 24 May at Hawthorn Quarries. The exercise was attended by local councillors, doctors, wardens, first aid men, N.F.S. and others who were given a practical demonstration of modern weapons. The spectators looked down from the grassy banks and watched the Home Guard attack a machine gun post, pouring round after round into it while the Commander and two of his men crawled to an embankment and hurled grenades at the machine gun post. There were demonstrations of spigot mortars, Northover projectors, Browning automatic rifles, Browning and Vickers machine guns, rifle grenades, 'sticky' bombs and the Sten gun. Also attending the demonstration was ex - Sergeant W. McNally of Murton who had won the Victoria Cross in the 1914 - 1918 war.

Seaham Colliery was on strike on Tuesday 26 May in a dispute affecting Putters. The Putters left the pit in the early morning because of a grievance about the score price in one of the seams. With the Putters away from their work, the Hewers and Fillers were obliged to leave the pit. A meeting that night decided the Putters had a case for an increase in the score price and the pit would remain idle.

Although 'Warship Week' had been a tremendous success it seemed to have had an adverse effect on subsequent savings afterwards. Savings scheme organisers called for the spirit of 'Warship Week' savings to be maintained in the future.

Recommendations of the Greene Committee on miner's pay was accepted by the War Cabinet by the middle of June. There was to be a minimum wage of 83s for all underground workers over 21 years old and 78s for surface workers. An unconditional flat rate of 2s 6d per shift for all workers over the age of 21 and all underground workers between 18 and 21 years old.

A Seaham man returned home to his parents on 22 June after being repatriated. Corporal Thomas Hope of the Royal Army Medical Corps whose parents, Mr and Mrs George Hope, lived at 'Valhalla' Camden Square, Seaham was one of the protected personnel with British prisoners of war repatriated from Italy.

While serving with the 8th Army in the Middle East at the beginning of the year he was captured while attending to the sick and wounded. He was attending in one of five ambulances that were moving slowly in a column in order not to distress the wounded. A Panzer column attacked with machine gun fire. Corporal Hope's ambulance was brought to a halt when a bullet burst a front tyre and others came through the vehicle. At this point the men were taken prisoner. They were sent to the nearest German dressing station where the R.A.M.C. looked after the wounded until they were taken to an Italian hospital. After ten days of looking after the wounded Corporal Hope went down with relapsing fever, a kind of malaria, and so was then sent to a German hospital that was based in Tripoli. He was treated for his illness for the next five weeks but he was the only British soldier in that hospital along with 150 German patients.

The R.A.F. were bombing the harbour in Tripoli causing some anxious moments especially when an ammunition ship was hit and blew up in the dock. On being discharged from hospital he was sent to a transit camp where there were about 300 British prisoners. As a serving Medical Corps serviceman he was classed as 'protected personnel' and was repatriated via Turkey. Corporal Hope praised the British Red Cross and the International Red Cross who so quickly returned him to his Motherland.

War has its own dangers but a constant fear among mining communities was that of underground explosions and so it was late on Friday night 26 June those fears visited Murton Colliery. An explosion in the five-quarter seam left thirteen men dead and a number injured. Heroic efforts were made by miners and officials to rescue the injured and get them to the surface disregarding their personal safety. One Putter found a fourteen year old boy, Samuel Abbott of Dene Terrace, crying out for help. This particular hero was Mr George Kirby Smith (30) of Toft Crescent, Murton. The lad was in a bad state so Mr Smith put him on his back and carried him half a mile through the fumes. "I'm burning, Geordie", young Samuel called out and Mr Smith found that the boy's clothes were smouldering. He tore off the clothing before carrying the boy the rest of the way to the landing. Mr Smith was treated in the ambulance room for multiple scratches caused by grit flying at velocity through the seam. There were five other miners suffering burns and shock.

The following Tuesday 30 June saw the sad internment of ten victims of the explosion. The burials took place in the new cemetery and the graves were laid side by side in one row. Conducting separate funerals in Holy Trinity Church were the Reverend W. H. Walton, acting vicar of Dalton-le-Dale and the Reverend S. Kearney, vicar of New Seaham. Well-known hymns were chosen by relatives and a full congregation was joined by groups from the management and the miner's union.

This year there was a call for everyone to stay at home for the summer holidays. The Ministry of Food decided that food that would normally be provided in factory canteens and the British Restaurant could be distributed to the public in the parks or on the beaches or other recreational places during the holiday week. Factory canteens were told that light meals could be served at these venues if canteen staff were willing to do this.

Girls at Murton Senior School sent a further £60 to buy rescue kits for the Merchant Navy Comforts Service making a total so far of £110. The Senior Girls had amassed £177 13s in cash and 506 garments were knitted. There was an Open Day at the school and this raised £7. The Headmistress, Miss E. Platts, thanked the girls for their tremendous effort.

Petrol shortages were responsible for the introduction of some strange modes of transport. One such vehicle seen in Murton was a polo-cart pulled by a smart dapple grey horse. The cart had six feet high wheels and high back seats.

Holy Trinity Church, Murton held a Memorial Service on Sunday 5 July for those who lost their lives in the Murton Colliery explosion on 26 June.

The National Fire Service was called out in the early hours of the morning on Saturday 4 July when a haystack belonging to Mr George Weightman, West Farm, Dalton-le-Dale was found to be well ablaze. The fire was soon brought under control by a trailer pump but not before a great deal of hay was destroyed.

A Seaham family was listening to a German broadcast on the wireless when they heard mention of a neighbour, Private Cook and that he was now a prisoner of war. The Cook family had not heard the broadcast and were asking if anyone else had heard the news to verify if the information was correct.

The funeral took place this Saturday of Leading Aircraftsman William Ross Graham (30) of Viceroy Street, Seaham who was accidentally killed while on active service in England. Members of L.A.C. Graham's unit attended the service at St. John's Church.

There was news this week of Fusilier W. Dyson whose name appeared in a list from German sources confirming that he was now a prisoner of war in North Africa. Fusilier Dyson (31) was the husband Mrs Dyson of 161 The Avenue, Deneside and he was serving with the Northumbrian Fusiliers. His last 'airgraph' to his wife was dated 23 May.

The Air Training Corps Seaham Squadron celebrated National Air Training Corps Sunday with a parade on 5 July lead by Flight Lieutenant J. C. Jennings. The 130 members of the corps attended a service in St. John's Parish Church. Messages of encouragement from Sir Archibald Sinclair, Minister for Air and Air Marshal Sir Charles Portal, Chief of Air Staff were read to the congregation.

The Ministry of Fuel ordered that householders were not allowed to order or acquire more than one ton of coal at any one time. This was to conserve coal stocks before winter set in.

There was a 'bring and buy' sale in Rock House on Thursday 16 July in aid of the Duke of Gloucester's Red Cross Fund. The sale was organised by Miss Nobbs of Sunderland and presided over by Miss Dillon. The sale raised £14. The fund was carrying out important work including care of prisoners of war by providing parcels of food and comforts for prisoners and also for helping relatives to visit their sick and wounded in this country. Since the beginning of the war the Red Cross had spent half a million pounds on parcels of food and comforts for prisoners of war.

In the second week of July the Seaham Detachment of the British Red Cross received a donation of £1 10s from the 'Spotters' of Frank and Grantham Avenue, Seaham who had raised the money by a penny a week subscription.

There were a number of weddings on August Bank Holiday in the area. At Murton Miss Gwen Thompson ignored superstition when she dressed for her wedding in a two piece costume of tan and lime green and carried a bouquet of cream roses. Bridesmaids were dressed in lilac-green and carried salmon coloured carnations. The Bridegroom was Leading Aircraftsman Nichol Jenning of Murton.

Seaham's 'Holidays at Home' began on Saturday 25 July with a number of events aimed at entertaining the town's folk throughout the two weeks. There were cricket matches, baby shows and domino competitions. An All-Star Concert Party held a show at the Spiritualist Hall and a whist drive was held at the British Restaurant in Adelaide Row, Seaham on Wednesday 5 August in the afternoon. There were thirty tables playing and Mrs T. Todd acted as M.C. and also presented the prizes. The recipients of prizes were Messes Meadows, Black, Campbell, Armstrong, Bell, Farrell, Mr. Reay & Mesdames Carling, Johnson, Clark and Ridsdale.

Seaham Council agreed to spend 1p in the pound from the rates (about £370) on attractions and amusements but this was subject to approval by the Ministry of Health. The holiday began on Saturday with a water carnival in the harbour with swimming races for boys, girls, men and women and also team events between the Forces, Civil Defence Forces, Police and National Fire Services. Additional items were life saving demonstrations, fancy and trick swimming and a comic event. Crowds of about 6,000 people made their way down the steps of the North Dock to enjoy an afternoon of fun.

On Sunday there were open air church services in Dawdon Dene Park for all denominations. The Children's Sunday School Service was held in the afternoon with an evening service for adults. The Salvation Army Band played the hymns and the combined church choirs led the singing of favourite hymns - Onward Christian Soldiers, O God Our Help in Ages Passed, Praise My Soul the King of Heaven, Eternal Father and Abide With Me.

Durham County Education Committee allowed the school playing fields in the town to be available for children's sports events. Cinemas arranged special films for the holidays and the Ministry of Information sent a mobile unit to show films of topical interest. It seems that even during the holiday period people were not allowed to forget that we were at war.

Chapter 4, 1942

One of the big successes was a paddling pool constructed on land that had been used formally by Coal and Allied Industries Ltd., off Dene House Road. It was built under the supervision of Council Surveyor Mr J. B. Abbey and many groups took part in its construction outside normal working hours. There were three water levels to accommodate children from tiny tots to primary school age. Civil Defence members gave their time to see that the children played safely in the pool and there were no accidents of note except for one small boy who lost his balance and fell full length in the pool fully clothed. Every day throughout the holiday saw the pool full of children.

Band concerts in Dawdon Dene Park provided a combination of entertainment and a beautiful setting equal to any of the usual holiday resorts. The rose gardens were at their very best and drew many favourable comments.

Laurence Kelly of 18 Candlish Terrace, Seaham was promoted to the rank of Squadron Leader in the R.A.F. this month. Squadron Leader Kelly was formerly a pupil at Ryhope Secondary School and then a student at Nottingham University. He was involved in research into aircraft construction.

Two Royal Airforce Stations took a hundred A.T.C. Cadets during the last week of July to show them how their operational stations worked.

Also in the last week of July an exercise in fuel assessment had gone terribly wrong. About 50% of forms that had been requested to be filled in had been incomplete and had to be returned to householders. The council had to fund the postage from the rates but the Post Office allowed the completed forms to be returned to the Fuel Overseer, Mr W. J. Dring, free of postage. The returned forms, about 500 in the first batch, had the questions that required answering marked in red. The householders had omitted to enter Identity Card numbers, the numbers of rooms in each house and the kind of lighting, electricity or gas.

St. John's Church Hall had a 'full house' and the audience enjoyed a programme of amateur dramatics by two groups. There were short plays such as, 'The Playgoers,' 'Mrs Feather's Fire' and 'Income Tax' by Mrs F. W. Armstrong's Amateur Dramatic Company. The Seaham Central Townswomen's Guild, Producer Mrs J. Gentles performed 'Mystery Cottage.' Alan Guy and his band completed the evening with a dance assisted by M.C.'s Dring, Potts, Foster and Goldsbrough.

There was to be a parade of military, civil defence and other units and displays on the Bank Holiday but this event was cancelled because of bad weather. A band concert was hastily arranged indoors by Dawdon Colliery Band and the band played a wide selection including some dance numbers.

Throughout the first week of August members of Murton and Dalton-le-Dale Scout Group spent the week under canvas at Startford. The scouts were under the supervision of Captain E. Irwin and Troop Leader Mr. N. Dargue.

Everything possible was done to make the 'stay at home holiday' a success and that is exactly what it was with the people taking part and enjoying every holiday event.

The enquiry into the explosion at Murton Colliery found that the explosion was caused by the firing of six shots simultaneously using the large exploder. The use of the large exploder on coal was said to be illegal and the appliance was intended only for use on stone drifts and not coal, whether in single shot or in series. It was illegal to fire more than one shot at a time.

It was learned this week that Private Harold Gorgenson of The Avenue, Deneside was now a prisoner of war in the Middle East. Pte. Gorgenson was serving with the D.L.I. More sad news arrived in Seaham at this time when official word was received by Mrs Milford of 217 The Avenue, Seaham that her son, Stoker John Ross Milford (26) R.N. was reported missing presumed killed on war service. It was also announced that Stoker J. H. Brown R.N. had lost his life at sea. He was the son of Mrs Frances Brown of 15 Dalton Avenue, Deneside. Stoker Brown also had two brothers serving in the Merchant Navy.

Councillor John McCutcheon, Librarian at Seaham Branch Library, received a letter in the first week of August from Miss Lettice Jowitt who was a former Warden of Rock House Educational Settlement. She told him that she was now working at an English Y.M.C.A. in the Middle East. She had just been talking to a Seaham man who had come into the building to buy some stamps and cigarettes. The North East connection was further extended when she related how she had tea recently with six Tynsiders.

Because of the serious state of things in Russia there were now calls being made for the opening of a second front by an invasion of Europe. The Communist Party members were urging this action but Britain was no where near ready for such action.

There was some concern that nursery units, set up by the Government to care for children under school age while mothers were working in factories, were not being used to the full extent as had been expected. The units were well equipped and staffed by experienced women and as the country was needing more and more women in the munitions factories and on the land the new nurseries would become very important by giving mothers the freedom to do such vital work.

A dancing display was held in the Dawdon Miner's Hall by Joan Tracy's Dance Troop early in August. Proceeds from the show went to Seaham Ladies Lifeboat Guild and the Mission to Seamen. The Lifeboat Guild received £7 and the Mission to Seamen £2 and both organisations expressed their thanks to Miss Tracy for her efforts.

The Reverend James Duncan was asked to undertake a lecture tour of Internment Camps that had been set up on the Isle of Mann. Organised by the British Council, the Reverend Duncan would stay for a week and give lectures of an instructive as well as an entertaining nature to those people who had been interned for the period of the war.

A public meeting in the Rex Cinema, Murton was aimed at instructing the people what was expected of them in the event of an invasion. However, perhaps because people felt

Chapter 4, 1942

that the likelihood of an invasion had passed the turnout was very poor. Speaking at the meeting, Mr R. T. Atkinson of the Ministry of Information said that there was a possibility that if Hitler could push back the Russian forces then he might yet try a snap invasion by something like 10,000 paratroops to pin down Bomber Command airfields. If this did happen then the Government was expecting that everyone would take up arms against the invader. Previous calls to 'stay put' had now been amended to 'stand firm.' It was felt that if an invasion was launched then the worst thing that the general public could do would be to flee from the enemy and so block the roads as had happened in places like Poland, Belgium and France. So, the word was now, 'stand firm.'

Another fine concert was performed in Murton on the Saturday evening 29 August by the 'Snappy Snappers' Concert Party. Proceeds from this event were forwarded to the 'Tank Week' effort. The keen youngsters had raised over £300 in 1942 for various charities with their excellent talents.

On Sunday 30 August the townspeople were advised to stay indoors during the morning as an exercise involving the R.A.F., the Home Guard and the Civil Defence would take place. Chalk bags were dropped, simulating bombs, from an Avro Anson aircraft as it flew at rooftop height along Jubilee Avenue and Mount Pleasant. Paratroops were also dropped but the umpires declared that the attackers were beaten off.

Mrs F. M. Gilmore, for the Seaham Detachment of the British Red Cross, graciously accepted the following donations to Red Cross funds. Dulcie Williams (9), Dorothy Miller (12), and Evelyn Purdy (13) the sum of £1 10s 6d proceeds of a jumble sale and competition held at Stewart Steet, Seaham. Margaret Wilkinson (10), Rutherford Avenue, New Seaham £2 the proceeds of a jumble sale. New Seaham British Legion per Mrs Wass, £1. Muriel Dixon (13), Alice Cole (13), Doris Nixon (6) and Jean Hedley (8), £3 the proceeds of a jumble sale and competition held at Grantham Avenue, Seaham.

The Ministry of Information arranged a very interesting talk on Tuesday 1 September in the Vane Tempest Miner's Welfare Hall. The speaker was Frau Irmgard Litten a German woman who gave a war commentary entitled, 'A Mother Fights Hitler.' The hall was crowded for this unusual and dramatic talk. Councillor H. F. Lee was chairman of the meeting and he was supported by Assistant Director, Ministry of Information, Newcastle, Mr M. Rowntree and Mr J. C. Edington, Secretary of the East Durham Committee. A vote of thanks was moved by Councillor J. H. Blackwell and seconded by Councillor Mr T. Todd.

Rock House was having something of a revival with the Sunday Evening Fellowship arranging lectures with such people as Mr Glen, National Savings Organiser who spoke on 'America' and Miss Anderson who arranged a musical evening under the auspices of the C.E.M.A. Miss M. Daniels of the County Drama Association and Miss M. Nobbs of the Sunderland Training College Hostel were due to speak later in the month. Sunday evenings here had been a popular venue for such events in the past and it was hoped that if sufficient numbers enrolled then perhaps a male voice choir might be formed.

At Seaham Magistrates Court in the first week of September a man from Frederick

Street was fined 20s for failing to obscure a house light. The Chairman of the Bench, Mr J. W. Claxton, said he would like to point out to the people of the town that the hours of darkness were longer now and that it was the responsibility of everyone to check that the blackout arrangements were in perfect order and showed no chink of light.

Other cases involved the none payment of water rates due to Sunderland and South Shields Water Company. The money owed ranged from 4s 7d to 17s 6d though it was reported that some of the money had been paid since the issue of the summonses. A number of people were also fined 6s for keeping dogs without a licence.

Moores Stores Ltd. was also in trouble for an infringement of conditions of sale. A customer had asked for a packet of jelly but was told by the manageress that she could not sell her the jelly unless she also bought a packet of semolina. The customer pointed out that it was an offence to impose such a condition of sale but the manageress said that was her instructions. Moores Stores Ltd. was fined £5 with £2 2s solicitors fees and 5s witnesses expenses.

A very unfortunate occurrence came about during an air raid on Saturday night 19 September. The altitude detonator of one of our own anti-aircraft shells failed and the live shell returned to the ground. It entered the upstairs back bedroom window of 13 Jubilee Avenue, New Seaham and exploded in the downstairs living room. The steel window frame of the living room was blown out into the front garden and severe damage was sustained to the house.

Mathew Davison (33) was killed instantly and Mrs Elizabeth Graham (52) was taken to hospital with serious injuries from which she later died. There were seven people in the house at the time including the children, Elizabeth Graham (10), Jean Davison (6) and Mary Ashett (5). Neighbours were quickly on the scene and some tried to gain entry to the house through the back door but the door was blocked with fallen masonry The emergency services were soon at work rescuing the occupants and the injured were soon taken to Sunderland hospital.

There were air raids most nights at this time all over the North East but this incident was a bitter blow to moral in the neighbourhood, one of those tragic accidents that happen from time to time.

A report from Church Army Headquarters to his family revealed that Captain Richard Neil of the Church Army had been wounded. Captain Neil had been in charge of Seaham Church Army Soldiers Club before going to serve in the Middle East as an Evangelist. He was in charge of a Church Army tea vehicle which was wrecked and he received a bullet wound in his knee. Before joining the Church Army he was a member of Christ Church Choir and also a Sunday school teacher. Captain Neil was the son of Mr Robert Neil of Ash Crescent, Seaham.

The drive to 'dig for victory' and produce more home grown produce was becoming more than just a leisure activity. Mr J. Elliott of 6 Glenhurst Terrace had been working to

Chapter 4, 1942

produce bigger tomatoes and this season had produced one of 1lb 2 1/2oz with a circumference of 13 inches.

At Dalton-le-Dale there was a presentation in St Andrew's Church when Mr C. Rutter, on behalf of members, presented Chinese book ends and a book to Miss Greta Spry who had been organist and Sunday school teacher for many years and who was leaving to go to college. There was also a presentation of a cheque to Mr W. Proud another church member who was leaving to join the R.A.F.

Miners and their families were now moving into new council houses at Parkside and Camden Square and other areas of redevelopment from clearance areas in New Seaham. Previously they only had to walk a short distance to their work at Seaham Colliery but might now have to travel up to two miles to work.

The Local Coal Production Committee were in talks with Northern General Transport in order to provide buses for miners to cover all three shifts with buses travelling from New Seaham to Seaham Harbour and to Parkside. The reason for this was to cut down on lost production time at the pits. From New Seaham to Seaham Harbour there would be a new twelve single journey ticket at a cost of 1s 6d and from New Seaham to Parkside the ticket would cost 2s 6d for twelve journeys.

Miners at Seaham Colliery, where there were no pit head baths, received their first allocation of soap off the ration in the second week of September. Each man received two six ounce tablets of soap intended to last three weeks; each tablet cost 3 1/2d. Supplies were delivered to the Colliery Office about every six weeks and as men drew this extra soap it had to be signed for and a card issued to every miner was punched.

Total National Savings in Seaham was now at £4312 and was made up of Savings Certificates £1664, Defence Bonds £1260, Savings Bonds £1000 and P.O. Savings Bank £388.

At Seaham Police Court three boys were fined £1 with 6s 8d costs after pleading guilty to stealing apples from the grounds of Seaham Sanatorium. Mr J. W. Claxton said that the offence was most serious because it concerned the food supply. With food in short supply throughout the country the 'scrumping' of apples could not be tolerated.

Seaham Ladies Hospital Guild reached its tenth year of fund raising for Sunderland Royal Hospital. Started in 1933, the group of twelve members under the chairmanship of Miss N. Dillon and the founder, Mrs J. W. Hall, Secretary, had raised approximately £500 for the hospital.

Scabies was becoming now more widespread in Seaham and there was concern that some people who had contracted this skin disease were not attending the cleansing centre for treatment. Moves were made to ask the Minister for Health to declare this disease a noticeable disease. It was an offence under the Scabies Order not to attend for treatment once a person had been sent a notice to attend for treatment.

The British Restaurant in Adelaide Row was having to put up notices to deter customers from walking off with cutlery from the restaurant. Councillor Mrs T. Todd said that the quality must be so good that people were taking a fancy to it.

People in the town were pressing for the London and North Eastern Railway Co. to open the service to Durham Elvet station again. The station at Seaton would be the link for Seaham and trains would run to Murton and Hetton and on to Elvet station. However, the company felt that there would not be enough passengers to make the service worth while and because of the need to conserve resources they turned the idea down. The service to Durham Elvet ceased in 1931 and trains now ran only from Pittington to Sunderland.

In early October the Ministry of Food began issuing a new quality dried egg powder for cooking. The price of the dried egg powder was 4s per pound and was only sold by grocers and provision merchants. A quick tasty meal could be conjured up mixing the dried egg with a little milk and frying it pancake style. Spread with strawberry jam this was a great favourite with children.

An unusual event occurred in Murton on 7 October. The story goes back to four years earlier when a young man, Hiram Brass, was unpacking a barrel of apples that had arrived from Nova Scotia, Canada. Hiram was getting his father's fruit shop stocked for the days trade on Woods Terrace. In the barrel he found a note asking for whoever opened the barrel and found the note to write as a pen-friend. The note was signed by young Jack Salsman of Nova Scotia. So, a friendship was kindled and both wrote to each other about their lives. When war broke out it was difficult to continue their correspondence of the last two years.

On Wednesday, Private Jack Salsman of the West Nova Scotia Regiment and now stationed somewhere in the south of England took a few days leave and arrived at Brass's shop in Murton and introduced himself as 'The Apple Barrel Kid,' the phrase he had first used in the note that he had placed in the barrel some years earlier. Pte. Salsman asked to see his friend Hiram only to be told that Hiram was now Leading Aircraftsman H. Brass and was serving with the R.A.F. in Egypt. Jack's journey was not in vain as he was made welcome by the people of Murton and made a number of new friends.

Flight Sergeant Albert Hoy, son of Mr and Mrs J. J. Hoy of Cedar Crescent, Parkside was recently promoted to his present rank. Albert Hoy had worked for the Co-operative Dairies before joining the R.A.F. He was now serving as a wireless operator in a bomber squadron. The 'Golden Caterpillar Award' was presented to him by a parachute company after he had to bail out of his badly damaged aircraft. On one occasion he returned to base in his Wellington bomber with most of his crew injured by flack.

The family of Private Alfred Kennedy received a photograph at their home in Frances Street, Seaham showing Alfred with other prisoners of war in Stalag 1XC in Germany. In the group photograph there was also a man from New Seaham by the name of Holby.

As the drive to produce yet more coal gathered pace the Durham Coal Owners Association agreed to offer miners 17s 6d per ton of coal if they would forfeit their allocation.

Chapter 4, 1942

The payments were free from income tax.

People in the area, who had just recently heard of the promotion of Flight Sergeant Albert Hoy, were shocked and saddened to learn that within a few days that he had been killed. Flight Sergeant Hoy was due home on leave in January and was to be married.

Also by the middle of October news had been received, at his home in Mount Stewart Street, Dawdon that Pilot Officer John Barritt was missing after a flight over Germany. John was formerly a choir boy in Dawdon Church. He was married there in September 1941 and had a baby daughter. Writing to P.O. Barritt's wife, his Commanding Officer described John as a first class airman and a courageous and distinguished comrade.

The Hon. Sec. of the Seaham Branch of the Soldiers, sailors and Airman's Families Association, Miss E. Marriner received a donation of £4 from Seaham and Dawdon T.W.G. as a contribution to the fund. Mrs F. M. Gilmore, Commandant of the V.A.D. received donations for the Red Cross Fund, Mr A. Williams of James Street, £5 5s, Elsie (13), Marjorie(9) and Mary Reed (11) of Foundry House, Seaham 11s 6d the proceeds of a jumble sale.

A Murton hero, Mr George Kirby Smith was honoured at the end of October by being told that he was to receive the Carnegie Trust Fund Certificate and £15 in recognition of his bravery in the Murton pit explosion on 26 June. Mr Smith of Toft Crescent rescued Samuel Abbott, a landing boy by carrying him half a mile on his back.

A Memorial Service was held on Sunday 25 October in Dawdon Parish Church for Flight Sergeant Albert Hoy. Flight Sergeant Hoy was killed in a flying accident in South Africa. The service was conducted by G. R. Berriman and the lesson was read by the Reverend James Duncan, Mr T. Stonehouse was at the organ.

Seaham Food Central Committee held a meeting to discuss a complaint against a woman who was said to have given her dog a plate of food in the British Restaurant in Adelaide Row, Seaham. The woman said that she had only given the dog scraps but a number of people believed the woman should be prosecuted. On this occasion the Committee decided not to prosecute but, as dogs were not allowed in the restaurant, if the woman went there again with her dog she would not be admitted.

On Tuesday night 3 November a talk was given by Mr R. Atkinson, an ex wireless operator in the Merchant Navy in the Vane Tempest Miner's Hall, Seaham. Given under the auspices of the Ministry of Information the lecture was entitled, 'The Battle of the Atlantic.' Mrs T. Todd presided over the meeting. Councillor H. F. Lee also brought up the question of unnecessary travel and full buses between Seaham and Sunderland. He said that women were not visiting Sunderland just for a day out but were travelling on Tuesdays and Thursdays for rabbits and fish and on Fridays for cakes. If there was better distribution of these foodstuffs to places like Seaham then it would help curb the extra travelling. The Committee agreed to bring the situation to the notice of the Regional Food Office.

Private Harold Gorgenson who had earlier been reported missing in action was now said to be a prisoner of war in Italy.

The three Londonderry owned collieries were exceeding their output target week in, week out. Miners in the town were making every effort to produce more coal that was so vital to the production of armaments. All the miners were 'doing their bit.'

The start of November was not the best start for the caretaker of the I.O.G.T. hut in Strangford Road, Seaham. He was last to leave the premises one night at 11.15 p.m. and had forgotten to switch the light off in the hut. At 5.30 a.m., P.C. Ord noticed the light burning and as there was no one on the premises realised that the light had been on all night. Seaham Magistrates concluded that this was simply an accident and hoped that more care would be taken in the future. The caretaker was fined £1.

Gunner John Scott (26) R.A. of 7 East Ellen Street, Murton was reported killed in action in Egypt. John was a former miner at Murton Colliery and was very well known as a boxer in the area.

Archdeacon Graham White, who had been vicar of Dawdon Parish Church from 1920 to 1925 was said to be with his wife in Singapore when the Japanese invaded. There was no news of their whereabouts at the present time.

Saturday 7 November saw the opening of the pithead canteen at Seaham Colliery. The opening ceremony was performed by the Marchioness of Londonderry. There had been temporary arrangements for miners to eat at the colliery but the new canteen, provided by the Miner's Welfare Committee, was a permanent arrangement and would provide hot meals at all times.

A forces wedding took place at Dawdon Parish Church on Sunday 8 November when Leading Aircraftswoman Isobel Davies, R.A.F. daughter of Mr and Mrs W. Davies of Melberry Street was married to Sergeant Alan Mason Pollock R.A.F. (Wireless operator/ airgunner) and son of Mr and Mrs J. M. Pollock of Camden Square, Seaham. The couple took leave and spent their honeymoon in Edinburgh.

Mr John H. Halliday, who was a sea going fireman, returned to his home at 80 Beech Crescent, Parkside, Seaham after his ship had been torpedoed in the North Atlantic. The commander of the German submarine which had sunk Mr Halliday's ship took the ship's captain on board the U-boat before casting the survivors off in two lifeboats. Speaking in good English the commander said, "Sorry boys, but war is war." The men were given a drum of drinking water and some cigarettes.

Nine of the ship's company were missing after two torpedoes had hit the ship but the two lifeboats, under the command of the first and second officers, got away with 24 men and 23 men respectively.

Mr Halliday said that the ship was struck by the torpedoes at about 10.30 a.m. while he was lying in his bunk. There were two terrific explosion which stopped the ship in its tracks and she began to take in water very quickly. One of the firemen was actually blown out of the stokehold and into the sea but he was rescued by men on the deck. Lifeboats were lowered taking on the survivors. The stricken ship went down in seven minutes.

Mr Halliday was in the boat commanded by the First Officer Mr R. W. Thompson of Park Crescent East, North Shields. It was Mr Thompsons great seamanship that saw them to safety. Without any navigation equipment he had to rely on navigating by the stars and steered towards an known port more than 6oo miles away. After four days the two lifeboats became separated and out of touch. Halliday's boat used sail for some of the time but were becalmed for two days when the men had to do rowing until a breeze gave them some more sail.

Most of the men were dressed scantily, Thompson had just a pair of pants and though the days were warm and tropical the nights were cold and the men had only small rations of water, biscuit and chocolate and the cigarettes given by the Germans soon ran out. There were so many in the boat that there was no room to lie down and after eight days they were all in an exhausted state. For several days the boat had been circled by sharks and this brought an added anxiety.

Finally, on that eighth day and only seven miles from land they sighted a ship and were delighted to be picked up and taken to George Town, Bahamas. There they were glad to see the crew of the other lifeboat which had also been picked up and taken to George Town.

The Carnegie Hero Fund Trustees announced at this time that they were awarding a certificate and £15 "to George Kirby Smith, a pit worker of Murton, Durham, who rescued a man following a colliery explosion." Few words indeed for a man who had upheld the traditions of miners throughout the centuries of helping injured colleagues to safety. The rescue had taken place on Friday night 26 June when after the explosion George Smith heard fourteen year old Sam Abbott shouting for help. Smith hauled Abbott onto his back to carry him out bye but the boy called out, "I'm burning, Geordie" and he dropped to the ground as his hands were so badly burned that he could not hold on to Smith's shoulders. Sam Abbott's clothing was found to be on fire so Smith tore the garments off the boy before again placing him on his back and holding him on he carried the boy for about half a mile to a place of safety. George Smith was treated in the ambulance room for cuts and scratches caused by the blast of small particles of stone which he described as being like small shot from a gun. Young Abbott spent a long period in the Royal Hospital, Sunderland and convalescence at Harrogate.

The people of Seaham were continuing to save towards the war effort and the savings for the week ending 7 November amounted to £768, Bonds £353, P.O. savings bank £612 making a total of £1,716. Considering the low wages in the town at this time these savings show the determination of ordinary people to do all that they could to help their country.

A lecture was given by Mr Charles Siddle of Sunderland when he spoke to a gathering at the Rock House Community Centre on Sunday evening 8 November. His subject was,

'Current Affairs'. Also this week a social evening was held in the Mill Inn by the New Seaham Womens' Section of the British Legion on Tuesday 10 November. There were more than one hundred members and their friend attending and enjoying the usual entertainment and the prize-winner for the evening was Mrs. Richardson.

A Memorial Service was held to the memory of Bombardier Thomas Wood R.A. (27), son of Mr and Mrs James Wood of 46 Ryton Crescent, Seaham. His death from illness in the Middle East was officially reported earlier. The service was held at Christ Church, New Seaham on Sunday 8 November. Bombardier Wood had been in the army for 8 years and had been awarded the Waziristan Campaign Medal. He had four brothers also serving in the forces, two in the Army and two in the Merchant Navy. Bombardier Wood's younger brother, Pte. Robert Wood (24) of the D.L.I. was a prisoner of war. A large congregation attended the service which was conducted by the Reverend S. Kearney.

Girls at Murton Senior School sent another £10 to the Merchant Navy Comforts Fund this week. Also at Murton a special Memorial Service was held at the Methodist Church by the Reverend D. W. Spedding. Hymns that had been specially selected by members of the church and who were now in the forces were sung and messages from them were read out to the congregation. A collection was held at the end of the service for the Army, Navy, Air Force and Seamen's Mission Comforts Fund.

The scourge of the killer disease Diphtheria was present in Seaham and other areas and the yellow 'fever ambulance' was to bee seen taking patients off to hospital. Immunisation against Diphtheria was being urged for all children with posters and newspaper advertising.

On Saturday 21 November there was a full house at the Empire Theatre, Murton to see the presentation of awards to Mr. George Kirby Smith. He was award a certificate and £15 from the Carnegie Hero Fund. This modest hero said in reply, "Thank you all. I was pleased to give service".

At a gathering in the Democratic Club Mr Smith received £50 worth of War Savings Certificates given by Murton miners and colliery officials and £5 by the South Hetton Coal Company. Young Sam Abbott received £5 from the Federation and £5 from the South Hetton Coal Company plus 10s from the Trimdon Grange Methodist Chapel as an expression of good will on his recovery from burns.

Because he had to go into hospital for an operation, Lord Londonderry, Chancellor of the University of Durham was unable to confer a degree on the Czechoslovakian President, Dr. Benes. Lord Londonderry underwent a successful operation for a hernia on Saturday. He was expected to stay in the London nursing home for about three weeks.

At Seaham Court on Friday 13, two men were fined for using a torch against regulations. The first man had a torch which, although it was of the right aperture it had been completely unscreened on the night in question. The second man was showing a bright light from a torch with an aperture of two inches and was also completely unscreened. In mitigation he said that his small son had the small torch and as he had just been to the pictures he thought

Chapter 4, 1942

that it would be all right to use the larger torch.

December started with a determined drive to collect as much scrap metal as possible starting on 7 December. Mr. V. L. McIntee, P.P.S to the Ministry of Works and Planning explained why this drive had come about. Previously most of the country's scrap metal had come from the U.S.A. but since that country had now joined the conflict America now needed all the scrap metal itself to produce armaments. Over the past twelve months, 1,600,000 tones of scrap metal had been collected using all the iron railings and steel from blitzed houses. As new arms factories came on line there was an even greater demand for metal. All farms, factories and collieries and such places would now have to look to see if there was any scrap metal that could be handed in. The collieries in County Durham had already handed over 50,000 tons.

The 'Beveridge Plan' was being discussed at this time and the scheme of Social Security outlined by William Beveridge was looked upon as the biggest step in insuring society from the pitfalls of everyday life. This National Insurance it was suggested would cost 4s 3d for men and 3s 6d for women per week. Everyone would be then insured from birth to burial, from cradle to grave. Benefits would be on a single stamp and all administration would be carried out by the Ministry of Social Security. Suppression of approved societies giving unequal benefit for equal contributions but retaining the Friendly Societies and Trade Union sickness benefits.

There would be suppression of the workmen's compensation and inclusion of special scheme for industrial accident and disease. There would be a comprehensive medical service for all.

Housewives would be a special class with marriage grant, maternity grant, widowhood and separation provision and a retired pension. The unemployment benefit would be at the full rate and indefinite subject to attendance at a training centre after limited unemployment. There was to be a weekly pension, other than industrial, on retirement and rising in value with each year of contribution after the minimum age.

The proposals seemed to be a good package and a step in the right direction for many people but there was a war to be won first and there would be much debate on the subject before the people would be able to give their approval at the ballot box.

A visit on, 1 December, of the Marchioness of Londonderry to the Girls Intermediate School in Station Road and to Camden Square School was an opportunity for Lady Londonderry to see the girls busy making garments for the children of members of the fighting forces under the 'Foster Parents Scheme of America.' Material was supplied by the American people and the school girls were working diligently and giving a great deal of their leisure time to this cause. Teachers also helped greatly by setting a high standard.

Lady Londonderry was accompanied by the Head Teacher Miss G. Lanther and watched the girls cutting out and sewing by machine and by hand and also some of the girls were knitting other garments. The girls at Camden Square School were among the first in the

County to carry out this work. Lady Londonderry congratulated the girls of both schools and said that the children of America were greatly interested in what was going on over here and interested in the children of England. Throughout County Durham 1,450 garments had been made up to date. The Marchioness hoped that at the end of the war children from Britain and America would exchange visits.

Also on Tuesday evening and under the auspices of the Ministry of Information, Miss Diana Wong gave a war commentary meeting at the Vane Tempest Miners Welfare Hall on 'The Battle Front in China.'

There was an appeal from the Railway Executive Committee not to send any parcels this Christmas as the railway has to move vital service personnel and weapons and munitions. Every available coach and truck was needed this Christmas.

'How Music Came into the Churches' was the subject of a talk given by Mr Jack Wick to Rock House Fellowship, Seaham on Sunday 6 December.

New Seaham W.I. agreed to give a Christmas gift of 3s to all husbands, sons and daughters of members serving in the forces. Mrs N. Southerland reported that £61 had been raised for charity over the past year and that 20 pounds of wool had been made into garments for sailors and sent to the Seaham Seaman's Mission. The evening ended with a talk on pottery given by Mrs. Deans of Murton.

A meeting in the Murton Democratic Club Hall of No. 6 Group of the Durham County British Legion decided to support a resolution to the County Meeting of Birtly, Dunston, Wardley and Heburn that the Ministry of Pensions be asked to abolish the Means Test applied to parents when making application for need pension in respect of members of the family killed while serving in His Majesty's Forces and that the Royal Warrant be amended to grant pensions to dependants for their loss.

Seaham War Services Fund organisers met in Dawdon Miner's Hall this Sunday. Funds had risen to record levels over the past twelve months and Mr. T. J. Curtis, Treasurer, said that more money had been handed over in the last twelve months than in the previous two years. The Dawdon Ward had raised a total of £1349 3s 3d which had been handed over to the parent body. £445 13s 6d had been raised by dances held in the Parish Hall. Whist drives held in the Miner's Hall had raised £185 10s 4d. There were four 'House to House' collections throughout the year bringing in £28 5s, £28 10s, £38 0s 2d and almost £33. There were also donations of £15 15s 11d including £7 received from Dawdon Bowling Club and £2 from Miss Tracey's Dance Class.

An inspection of the 12th Cadet Battalion of the Durham Light Infantry on Sunday saw 422 officers and men taking part. The Battalion was just formed in June and the Inspecting Officer, Col. A.L. Scott-Owen, congratulated the men on their smart appearance, keenness and alertness on parade.

There was much concern that not enough children were being brought forward to be immunised against Diphtheria. Dr. R. J. Hetherington, Medical Officer for Seaham said that we should not be satisfied until at least 80% of the towns children had been immunised; the case for immunisation was overwhelming.

There had been 210 cases of Diphtheria in Seaham up to the end of October and of this number only 11, or 5% had been immunised and 191, or 88% had not. There were seven deaths and these patients had not been immunised. The cost to the community for the care of 200 patients with Diphtheria was something in the order of £4,000 whereas the cost of immunising this same number was only a few shillings.

At this time there were about 30% of children under five and about 60% of children of school age who had been effectively immunised. Children under five were the most vulnerable group to catch the infection. Clinics for the immunisation against Diphtheria were opened at 1 Princess Road on Friday afternoons and Saturday mornings and also at the Child Welfare Centre.

A most unusual case came before Seaham Juvenile Court on Monday when a fifteen year old youth from Murton was charged with malicious damage after he through a Mills Bomb down the pit shaft at Murton between 10 and 10.30 a.m. on 4 September. He was also charged under the Defence Regulations with throwing a bomb with the intent to impede the working of machinery used in the performance of essential services and further with throwing a bomb into the shaft believing it would be likely to interfere with those working below on essential service.

The youth, who was an apprentice electrician, had been working in the vicinity of the Middle Pit shaft when an explosion took place which caused damage which cost up to £30 to repair. When questioned by police the youth said that he did it because he was sick of his work. After further investigations the youth was further charged with sending misleading telephone calls in June, August and September reporting false air raid warnings. These calls put the Civil Defence and Police to a great deal of trouble at a time when the North East was going through a period of many night time air raids. The defendant was committed for trial to Durham Quarter Sessions.

Speaking at a meeting of the Seaham Divisional Labour Party on Saturday 5 December, Mr Emanuel Shinwell spoke of the Beveradge Report and said that it was satisfactory as far as it went but that it would not address the underling problems of poverty. He agreed that it would bring a measure of relief but that those who would benefit from the scheme would still remain in a condition of poverty so long as the present economic system remained.

Mr. Shinwell continued, "The Capitalists can safely sleep in their beds. The scheme will not disturb them or reduce their standard of life. The wealthy will remain wealthy and the poor will remain poor; class distinction will continue and the ramp of private profit making will persist. We shall accept it and, indeed, must see that everyone accepts it but much more than this is required before the Labour Movement can be satisfied."

At the same meeting Mr V. K. Krishna-Menou, Secretary of the Indian League, spoke of the people of India and their determination to beat Fascism. There was no truth he said in the idea that any section of the Indian population would favour a Japanese victory. However, he did feel that the resistance of Fascism should be allied with Independence. The vast majority of Indian workers and peasantry could not escape the horrors that assailed them until there was a National Government in India, elected by the Indians and responsible to the Indian people.

Seaham Spotters Club held tests this week and presented certificates of qualification to R. Elgey, M. Bainbridge, M. Hillam, S. Horn and G. Smith. The Spotters Club formed a vital part of the air raid defence organisation.

Seaham National Fire Service was called out to a fire on Wednesday night 9 December in a house in Viceroy Street where an electric iron had been left on the floor. The iron had burned through the floor boards and caused a small fire which the owner had partially extinguished but the Fire Service completed the job making the premises safe again.

The Washing Plant at Murton Colliery was under fire from local people concerned about the state of the Dawdon Dene beck and the pollution of the water by the washing process at the pit. The stream was now flowing with a black-gray slime and the water mark was clearly visible along the banks. No wild life exists in the water and this was spoiling an otherwise beautiful natural vale.

A man from Murton was fine £5 at Seaham Magistrates Court for stealing live rabbits, three Flemish Giant does worth £1 each and one English doe worth 10s. Magistrates viewed the offence as very serious at a time when the public were being urged to rear rabbits to augment the food ration. There would be no incentive to do this if hutches were being raided and rabbits stolen.

On Tuesday night there was a fatal accident when Mr. John Willis was killed by a fall of stone while working in the No.2 Hutton Seam. Mr. Willis, who was forty two years old, lived in Viceroy Street, Seaham.

At Seaham 'Wesley' Methodist Church in Tempest Place the Choir and friends performed Handel's 'Messiah' on Saturday evening 19 December. The principals being Madame Edna Eales (soprano), Miss Margarete Topping (contralto), Mr. Jack Wick (tenor) and Mr. T. W. Leighton (bass). The organ was played by Mr. G. Green and the orchestra was conducted by Mr. T. C. Littledyke. The proceeds from the concert were given to the Trust funds.

Carol services were held on Sunday 20 December and also on 27 December at 6 p.m. at St. John's Parish Church and on Christmas Eve there was a carol service and midnight Christmas Communion. St John's Sunday School 'Open Day' was held in the afternoon of the 20 December in the school hall. The children entertained guests with a Nativity play and other Christmas items.

At Dawdon Parish Church on 27 December there was an evensong known as 'Service of Carols and Nine Lessons' which was a tradition of King's College, Cambridge and also of Eton College Chapel. The Reverend G. R. Berriman, helped by Mr. T. Stonehouse, took the choir through rehearsals over the past few weeks and the congregation enjoyed the service which had such a Christmas tide appeal.

For gallantry and devotion to duty, a Bar to the D.F.M. was awarded to Flight Sergeant Robert Langlands Turner (21) a wireless operator and air gunner of 97 Bomber Squadron of the R.A.F. He had recently flown in attacks on the Genoa raids and Milan as well as raids over Germany. He had been awarded the D.F.M. in January, 1941 and on that occasion he was presented with a wrist watch by Seaham Urban Council and a silver cigarette case was presented to him by residents of Corcyra Street and other friends. He had been on 74 operations against the enemy to date.

A troubled year was now drawing to a close. Night time air raids had been common throughout the year and loss of life had brought grief to a number of local families. There were many sleepless nights which meant that people were going to work tired and children were having to go to school after having been disturbed in their sleep perhaps two or three times during the night.

Shortages of just about everything were a big problem, particularly food. Those children who helped their mothers by going to collect their families rations from the store that they were registered with sometimes had to wait for perhaps two hours for the butter to arrive - from where, they never knew.

However, the good people of Seaham and Murton got on with it. They helped themselves and they helped each other and under trying conditions they attempted to make it the best of all worlds.

Chapter 5, 1943

Some Optimism Begins to Surface

A whist drive was held for the patients of Seaham Hall Sanatorium on New Year's Eve followed on New Year's night by a wonderful evening of entertainment. A concert party, lead by Mr. Bates of South Shields, cheered everyone up with a presentation of the famous Tommy Handley radio show 'ITMA.' Besides the comedy takeoff of 'ITMA' there were also other items of songs and comedy.

The Seamen's Mission gave a dinner to the officers and men of the Merchant Navy on New Year's day. Seasonal fare was provided in the form of turkey, rabbit and Christmas pudding. A local battalion of soldiers was specially invited to the dinner and the guests enjoyed games and dancing after the meal.

There was a dance arranged by 'B' Company of the Home Guard on New Year's night in the Drill Hall, Seaham. There was a whist drive organised by Sergeant Major Bynam and Sergeant Slater and the dancing was organised by Sergeant Crozier and Sergeant Rudkin. Music was provided by Alan Guy and his band.

On 3rd January St. Mary Magdelen's Youth Movement gave an entertainment to patients at Seaham Hall Sanatorium. The entertainment consisted of a Nativity Play by the girls and a musical interlude by Miss Sheila Kirby of Murton. There was also an operetta, 'Silence in Court' performed by the boys and girls.

Another New Year party was held in the Conservative Club on Tuesday 5 January and presided over by Mrs G. Balls. There were games and dancing which had been organised by Mrs. B. Weatherall and Mrs. C. Murray. Other entertainment was provided by Miss. Outred. The annual children's party was dispensed with this year but each of the children received a war savings stamp.

At the suggestion of some members of the Rock House Committee, pensioners who attended the social evenings were invited for a night out to the Empire cinema at the invitation of Mr. J.C. Harrison, Manager. The film shown was 'Tarzan in New York' which the group thoroughly enjoyed.

It was announced on the 13 January that the call up age for all single girls was to be lowered to 19 years old.

The Mosquito squadron based at Acklington scored its first kill on Thursday 21 January.

Chapter 5, 1943

A Dornier Do127 was brought down near Hartlepool.

Girl pupils attending Dawdon Junior School sent a donation of £7 10s to the Merchant Navy Comforts Service.

Mr. Arthur Greene of Heighington was described by Mr. Will Lawther, President of the Mineworker's Federation of Great Britain, as the greatest living expert on coal. Mr. Greene was seeking the co-operation of the mining community in County Durham, Mr. Lawther and miner's M.P.'s and also leaders in the Government to draw up a scheme initially to bring forward the inspection and surveying of all Durham collieries and that for this purpose funds should be made available. The scheme would be wide ranging and, when the report was complete, would be handed to the appropriate Government Authority.

In the New Year Honours List it was revealed that Seaham man, Mr. Michael Ernest Frost, who had served in the Merchant Navy all his life has been awarded the British Empire Medal, Civil Division. Mr. Frost was born in Tolsbury, Sussex but had lived in Seaham since he was a boy. At this present time he was serving in the steamer 'Nephrite.'

Sergeant Arthur Staff (27), an Observer/Navigator in the R.A.F. whose family live in 38 Calvert Terrace, Murton, was reported missing after air operations over enemy Germany. Sergeant Staff had been recently home on leave and had only reported back to duty two days before being posted missing. Also from Murton, Sergeant Richard Cook (19) R.A.F. of Porter Terrace was reported missing after operations over enemy territory. He was the only son of Mr. and Mrs. R. Cook.

A Dalton-le-Dale man, Private Thomas Finkell Watson, D.L.I. who lived at 8 Dunelm Terrace,

was reported to be a prisoner of war in the hands of the Italians. He had been reported as missing in the Middle East.

The Murton boy who threw a Mills bomb down the shaft at Murton Pit was bound over in the sum of £50 to be of good behaviour.

Twelve year old Miss. Edith Dodds, working on her own initiative was busy making flowers from coloured paper the sale of which raised £10 for the Merchant Navy Comforts Fund. Edith lived at 35 Forster Avenue, Murton and she expressed a wish that the money she had raised should go to provide rescue kits for the seamen. This was her fifth effort at raising money in this way and in recognition of this she was presented with a service badge. The girls at her school, Murton Senior Girls School, had so far raised £234 17s 9d and dispatched 600 knitted garments.

At the Seaham Council meeting on Tuesday 26 January, grave concern was expressed about the amount of thefts and damage to air raid shelters. It was decided to place the matter in the hands of the police and to ask for the co-operation of the public to report any evidence of theft or vandalism.

Some Optimism Begins to Surface

Shovels, pails and spades had been stolen from shelters to the value of £40 and 300 locks had been either stolen or damaged and had cost nearly £60 to replace. A new bed had been taken from a bunk in one shelter and other beds had been damaged besides light bulbs and cable. There had been complaints that shelters were not opened soon enough but there was a feeling that this was hardly surprising given the problems that the Council were faced with.

Also at this Council meeting recommendations of the British Restaurant Committee, subject to approval by the Ministry of Food, it was agreed that a branch restaurant be established in the Deneside Housing Estate. The restaurant would start with meals provided on a cash and carry basis to begin with then, if the project was viable, other meals would be considered in the future. Mrs. J. Todd, Chairman of the Restaurant Committee, said that the Seaham Restaurant had not only paid its way since its inception but had also made a little profit which would go to provide an even better meals service.

Ralph Ellwood of Murton, who played football for Murton Colliery Welfare scored five goals against Blackhall Methodists in a Seaham and District League match on Saturday 6. This young man was catching the eye of other clubs as he had had such a very good season scoring 49 goals in 21 games. He had three games in trials for Newcastle United in which he had scored three times.

The new rationalisation of milk distribution began on Sunday 7 February. The scheme was aimed at saving manpower, transport, petrol and tyres. Most people would be supplied by their usual trader but in some cases another trader would be delivering their milk. Customers were assured that no one would be without their normal supply.

Seaham Amateur Operatic Society was now into its thirty fourth production in staging the pantomime, 'Dick Wittington,' at the Theatre Royal for one week starting on the 8 February. The producer of the show was Mr. Jack Hylton of South Shields who had produced the last four pantomime productions and the music was by Mr. Stan Hunter with Miss M. Hunter at the piano.

Work on the new Murton Colliery canteen was going ahead and was expected to be officially opened some time in April. The cost of the canteen would be over £3,000. In the case of the pit head baths it was reported that total income was £1,819 and expenditure was £2,210 leaving a deficiency of £391.

Lieutenant J. G. Blenkinsopp R.A., the son of Mr. and Mrs. A. Blenkinsopp of 2 North Doxford Terrace, Murton was awarded the Military Cross after a battle in the Libyan desert. Lieut. Blenkinsopp's tank had been in the thick of the action about a hundred yards from the German lines when a piece of shrapnel caught him in the leg and shattered the bone. His crew managed to get clear of the immobilised tank while he crawled to a nearby shell hole but was again hit by shrapnel.

He was now losing a great deal of blood but was able to stem the flow by using his lanyard as a tourniquet, tightening it with the barrel of his pistol. Machine gun fire was sweeping the area so Lieut. Blenkinsopp had to lie low for almost five hours before being rescued. He was finally rescued by Lance Bombarder W. Potts who carried him 600 yards to safety. Throughout the five hours in the shell hole, Lieut. Blenkinsopp continued to send information back to H.Q. until a bullet wrecked his radio.

On Sunday night 14 February, the Youth Fellowship met in Dawdon Parish Hall to debate the question, 'The woman's Place is in the Home.' The debate concluded that 'Woman's Place was in the Home' by a vote of 33 to 3. In another debate they also concluded that 'It was better to be wise and poor than ignorant and rich.'

At the beginning of the week, William Adamson of 47 Toft Crescent, Murton took a look at the egg production of his Black Wyandotte hen and decided that she was not doing her bit for the food supply and would therefore have to face the axe later in the week. The bird must have taken the threat seriously because by the Wednesday when Bill went to feed the hens he found that the Wyandotte had produced a huge egg of five ounces. This was followed by another large egg of three and three quarters and by the weekend was laying normal sized eggs. The death penalty was therefore lifted and the bird would not now be making an appearance on the dinner table.

The Thomas Tilling Group were now equipping United Automobile buses with gas trailers so saving on liquid fuel. There were 107 buses converted up to the present and had saved a quarter of a million gallons of liquid fuel. However the power output of such vehicles was very poor and when the Northern buses were converted, those leaving the Castlereagh bus stop in Seaham often had to be given a push in order for the vehicle to take the gentle uphill gradient past the Drill Hall.

The Seaham Food Committee meeting on Monday 1 March received a letter from the Northern Divisional Food Office in reply to their complaint about the shortage of fish. The complaint seemed to have produced some action as since the last meeting fish supplies had improved. There was also discussion about the case of a woman who suffered from rheumatoid arthritis and who had been getting her milk from a local farm but since the new regulations came into force she had had her milk supplies transferred to another retailer. She had written to Lord Woolton (Minister of Food) about this after hearing on the radio that milk could be bought from the old retailer if the milk was collected by the customer.

However, the Minister replied that this had been a mistake and that milk could only be bought from the retailer that had been given the registration transfer. Counc. W.P. Smith said that the woman felt that the farm milk was better for her condition and that as she was being given gold injections the combination seemed to be doing her more good. He said that other people may be in a similar position and that there could be a case for changing these rules on medical grounds. Mr. Smith moved that this should be put before the Divisional Officer and this motion was carried. One other problem was expressed about milk being delivered in churns and milk being ladled out to customers in stead of being delivered in bottles.

Some Optimism Begins to Surface

The Seaham Girls Training Corps which was formed in June 1942 now had 71 members. Most of the girls were pupils at Seaham Secondary School and there were also a number of sixteen to seventeen year olds, past pupils of the school and who were now employed in various occupations. The girls had received excellent training including company drill, fire fighting and dispatch carrying. During the present term the girls were being trained in the 'Handy Woman's Course' which included such things as packing a suit case, polishing shoes, patching and darning, putting a new washer on a tap and cleaning a gas oven. A course on the internal combustion engine was also arranged with the co-operation of the A.T.C.

For recreation the girls enjoyed Scottish Country Dancing and also, jointly with the A.T.C. held a monthly dance. Parades held in the Seaham Intermediate Girls School on Friday evenings between 7 - 9 p.m. also had interesting lectures by members of the armed forces.

By the middle of the month it was learned that Corporal S. Hall (23) D.L.I. of Wetherburn Avenue, Murton who had been reported as missing was now known to be a prisoner of war in Italian hands.

On Thursday and Friday 11 and 12 March the North East suffered a very heavy air raid and a number of incendiary bomb clusters were dropped west of Seaham.

Members of Murton Holy Trinity and St. Andrew's Church, Dalton-le-Dale would not be having an annual outing this year but instead were entertained to a film matinee in the Rex Theatre on Saturday 13 March. There was a good turn out for the show and among the films shown was, 'Queen Victoria' which was shown in Technicolor.

Also on Saturday afternoon Mr. Emanuel Shinwell spoke to a meeting of Seaham Division Federation of Labour Women's Sections at the Miner's Hall, Murton. He was putting forward his views on the Beveridge Report to a large and attentive audience. "It is significant," said Mr. Shinwell, "that Sir John Anderson and Sir Kingsley Wood are silent about the Beverage Report. The defence of the Governments attitude is left to a Labour member of the War Cabinet. No doubt some members of the Government would be pleased if the report was to be forgotten. Unfortunately for them it is still very much alive and a great deal more would be heard about it in the future.

I have no patience with those people who say it does not go far enough. Of course it is limited in its scope and it does not pretend it is a panacea from all our ills but it does lay the foundations of Social Security by removing actual want and providing a minimum standard. I also agree that it requires amending but that it the function of Parliament and we can tackle it as soon as the Government is ready to produce the necessary legislation.

I notice that the Young Tory Group in Parliament have put down a motion asking for a Minister of Social Security. That is strange because they demanded the same during the recent debate but when it came to a vote after the Government declined to accept their amendment they ran away and voted with the Government. That was an exhibition of political cowardice of the worst kind and now they return to the attack when everybody knows it is just window dressing. There is only one thing worse than a die-hard Tory and that is a young Tory who pretends to be advanced in his ideas but is really only a little more astute than his grandfather.

The actions of some of these gentlemen is bringing Parliament into disrepute. It is no use saying it takes time to produce legislation on the subject. If it was a Bill to ensure compensation of labour it would be passed in a single day."

Night time air raids continued almost every night and this week saw many magnesium parachute flares descending over the area as bombers searched out their targets. Low flying tactics were being used by Dornier aircraft to avoid being picked up by Chain Home radar stations. One Dornier flew very low over Seaham in the early evening and had to climb sharply to avoid houses at Mount Pleasant. It was not until the raider had passed over Seaham that the air raid warning was sounded.

St. Patrick's Day was observed by Murton St. Joseph's Church with Mass being conducted by the Reverend W. Conway and Shamrock was distributed to the members of the church. There were fancy dress dances for the infants and juniors and a social evening was held by the church women's organisation later.

At this time the miners were asking for new compensation rates in both fatal and nonfatal accidents. The rate at the time was 30/-s a week plus 5/-s war bonus for single men with an addition of 5/-s for each child in the case of a married man. The Government was being asked to set a rate 50% more than this in order to set a reasonable standard of living so that this would help to restore men quickly to good health again and to their essential work.

A Murton man, ex - miner Able Vardy, who had been employed as a horse keeper at Murton Colliery twenty years ago, died this week at Houghton. He was head of a successful haulage company and coal merchant with his two sons. The younger son was farming at East Boldon and the eldest, Mr. Reg Vardy controlled the management of the business.

The British Red Cross has told relatives in Seaham, whose sons or husbands are prisoners of war in the hands of the Japanese, that letters to their men folk should be typed or printed. If this was not done then it was unlikely that their letters would pass Japanese censorship.

Mr. Thomas Dale of 8 Ranksborough Street, New Seaham had poems published on 2 April showing how he felt about the war and about the sweeter things in life. He was inspired to put down on paper his thoughts about a recent air raid in the South when air gunners in a German bomber strafed a school playground.

> From one hundred feet the
>   ground is near,
> And they can see the people
>   clear.

Some Optimism Begins to Surface

Gunner grinning like a fool,
Saw children playing round their school.
Then with guns gave them a blast.
Laughed and said, "You've played your last.
O'er the school they then did pass,
Death had come to this whole class.
To say all we think is out of our power,
To see little buds cut before they could flower.
Go over there, start up a ruction,
But not with juvenile destruction.
Strafe Berlin with your greatest raid,
Come back and whisper, "With our aid,
Children, now your debt is paid."

Thomas Dale also loved to write about nature and the following poem shows the delight that he found in the simple things in life.

While I was in the garden weeding,
And looking after cabbages seeding.
I also noticed near a bush,
That songster bird they call the Thrush.
Then lifting high his head I heard,
The sweetest music from that bird.
Exalted, yes my spirit did rise,
I would not move him to his surprise.
Let God's good gifts pour forth in song,

> May they last both clear and
>   long.
> Standing so near, amazed, yet
>   thrilled,
> Oh when he finished the air
>   seemed stilled.

Thomas, a native of Carlisle, had moved to Seaham in the early thirties and worked at Vane Tempest colliery.

'Wings for Victory Week' began on April 10 in Seaham and continued until 17th. The target was £75,000 and with the great success of 'Warship Week' to measure by it looked as though this effort would also inspire the townsfolk to double their endeavours. It was known that there were about 760 people from the Seaham area who were now serving in the R.A.F. so a great many families were interested in seeing this campaign provided much needed funds for the service.

Auxiliary Forces opened the 'Wings Week' with a parade through Seaham. These included men and women and boys and girls of these services and the numbers taking part were an indication that they looked forward to a great victory. Even an Old Age Pensioner Group meeting in Rock House held a sale under the 'free gift scheme' of things they had made and vegetables they had grown.

There were many entertainment's in connection with 'Wings Week' such as a special show of films at the Princess Theatre on Wednesday afternoon and an arts and crafts exhibition in Rock House Community Centre. There was also a whist drive there aimed at raising more funds for 'Wings Week'. A children's entertainment was held in St. John's Parish Church Hall and arranged by Mrs. F. L. Armstrong and performed by local children including pupils of Miss Violet Oughtred and Miss Joan Tracy. This event had 'standing room only and the large audience enjoyed the show immensely.

The A.T.C. held an open night at their headquarters in Dene House Road and North Road. The public saw the cadets at work and the training facilities available to them. The A.T.C. had been formed two years previously and on its second birthday, Thursday, they held a boxing tournament. The squadron had 200 personnel with 9 officers, a Warrant Officer and six instructors.

Byron Terrace Girls Club gave an evening of entertainment arranged by Miss M. Barkess in the New Seaham Conservative Club.

One of the fund raising efforts was a 'mile of pennies' which was set up along The Avenue, Deneside. Stencilled aircraft were displayed on the paving stones over the mile from the bottom of Deneside to Mount Pleasant.

On Thursday, girls from Seaham Secondary School performed the play 'Macbeth' by William Shakespeare. Macbeth was played by Janet Coxon, Lady Macbeth by Jean Curry,

Banquo by Phylis Wheatley and Macduff was played by Vera Storey. Other characters were, the three weird sisters played by Sheila Vipond, Doreen Leslie and Elsie Pigg. The role of the drunken porter was played to perfection by Betty White. All the girls were complimented on their great performance. A collection during the interval raised £12 8s 6d and was contributed to the 'Wings for Victory Week.'

Mrs. W. Spry of 1 Murton Street, Murton received official word this week that her son, private James N. Spry (30) D.L.I. had been killed in action in Tunisia. Pte. Spry was a well known sportsman in the area and played centre-half for Murton Colliery Welfare F.C. when they were in the Wearside League.

The wages for Deputies in the Durham Coalfield were raised this week by 1s per shift bringing their wage up to 18/1.7d per shift.

During the third week of April it was expected that First Class Stoker, Stanley Hall would be returning to his home from an Italian prisoner of war camp but he was not in the first batch of exchange prisoners. Stoker Hall of Adolphus Street, Seaham had been in the Navy for nine years and was serving in a British submarine in 1940 when it was sunk and he was taken prisoner. His letters from Sulmona Camp in Italy had been cheerful and it was now believed that he would be back at his home in about six weeks.

On Tuesday 20 Mr. H. F. Lee, Chairman of Seaham Savings Committee gave a report on the outcome of the 'Wings for Victory Week.' The target had been set at £75,000 but the town really set about the task with alacrity and the amount actually raised was £103,247. There had been three 'Weeks' since the beginning of the war and the Seaham district had raised nearly a quarter of a million pounds. Mr. Lee pointed out that Seaham was not a wealthy community but the response from the town had been magnificent.

Every organisation in the town had contributed to the 'free gift scheme' and this single item of fund raising had brought in £900. Customers of local banks saved a total of £35,000 which underlined the importance of small savers at this time. Small contributions such as half a crown from old age pensioners all helped the cause and there were donations from Yorkshire and Lancashire former residents of the town who sent ten shilling notes and asked to be associated with the town's 'Wings Week' and two pound notes arrived on the last day of the week from two old people who wished to see the target exceeded. In concluding Mr. Lee said, "It was gifts like these which showed the spirit of the people and that their fine total stood well in the eyes of the country."

At the beginning of May Mr. Arthur Greene published his report on the 'Oil from Coal' idea. The cost of a complete plant which would treat two tons of coal per hour or fifty tons a day was quoted as £27,000. The plant would be complete in itself and no further ancillary machinery would be required. The raw coal or shale would go into the hopper at one end and would be crushed, pulverised and retorted, the gas given off would be condensed and refined and the motor spirit and diesel oil would run out separately at the other end. This would make great savings on importation of oil from abroad.

Mr. Hugh Dalton M.P., President of the Board of Trade spoke at a May Day meeting in Durham on Saturday 30 April in the Miner's Hall. He recalled that two years ago the miners of County Durham had purchased two Spitfires for the country and in so doing gave a lead to the country which was now being followed by 'Wings for Victory Week.' That gift was typical of the spirit of the miners in the face of dangers and adversity. "I have in my office at the Board of Trade a photograph of the plaque which commemorated your gift and I often show it to American and other visitors to indicate to them what kind of people you are."

From the 10 May and for one week the film, 'In Which We Serve' was being shown at the Empire Theatre staring Noel Coward and John Mills. This story of a Destroyer is one of the great wartime sea films and was well attended by local people. The film gave a graphic account of the war at sea, something that most of the people of Seaham could relate to.

The Reverend James Duncan reported that Mrs. Graham White, wife of Archdeacon Graham White of Singapore, former vicar of Dawdon, was alive. She had been reported as being killed when the Japanese invaded Singapore. A telegram had been received from Tokyo at the British Red Cross Headquarters that Mrs. White was alive and interned at Changi. There was no news of the Reverend White though there was a large number of people who were not listed and therefore could still be alive.

There was a heavy air raid on the Saturday night 15/16 May when Dornier bombers flying from their base in Soesterburg, Holland attacked targets in east Durham and Sunderland. Parachute flares were seen around Seaham as enemy aircraft lined up their target. This may have been the Seaham Docks or Vane Tempest Colliery. Propaganda leaflets were also dropped in the area at this time giving exaggerated claims of British shipping losses.

At 2 a.m. two Observer Corps men, Tom McNee and Billy Whitelock were on duty at the top of St. John's Church tower when a huge parachute land mine drifted down and exploded in the very densely populated area to the south east of the church. A house in Adolphus Street West was destroyed and Mr. George Kennedy (75) and Mr. Charles Young (31) were killed. Special Police were soon on the scene to rescue others of the family including baby Janette Young who, though covered with blood, had not actually been injured.

In Sophia Street more houses were destroyed and six people lose their lives. The dead were Hilda Gaut (22), Michael Richard Hughes (49), Doreen Hughes (9), George Kelly (61), Margaret Kennedy (73) and Joseph Nicholson (54).

Viceroy Street took the brunt of casualties with many houses destroyed. Those killed included Lily Wilde (24), George William Weir (43), Elizabeth Walker (55), Jenny Walker (18), Phylis Miller (45), William Henderson (10), Joan Henderson (9), John Dobson (32), Georgina Dobson (31), Joyce Dobson (4), John Thomas Davison (35), Wrightson Kirk Cuthbert (28), Gerald Corkhill (36), Barbara Dixon Corkhill (29), Alan Corkhill (6), Marion Corkhill (4), June Corkhill (1), John Bell (35) and Irene Appleton (8).

Some Optimism Begins to Surface

The injured were quickly taken to hospital in Easington and Ryhope. At Leeholme Hospital five of the injured died. They were Violet Daisy Shaw (54), Vincent Oglesby (41), Richard Nixon (76), John Kelly (48) and Thomas Henry Grange (79). At Thorpe Hospital, George Harrison Hall (16) died of his wounds and at Ryhope Hospital, Mary Kelly (19) also lost her fight for life.

At 2.15 a.m. two parachute mines fell at Old Burdon but failed to explode however the B1404 road had to be closed until the next day when the mines were defused. Also at this time a heavy explosive bomb fell at New Seaham which slightly damaged some houses. At 3 a.m. one of our own ack-ack shells fell to the ground and damaged a house in Seaham.

The scene in Camden Square School where the homeless and walking wounded were temporarily being sheltered was a sombre place with people talking quietly among themselves. Some had heads bandaged others with arms in slings. 102 families had lost their homes but Government working with Billeting Officers found places for 1,200 people.

Viceroy Street Infants School was badly damaged as was the National School. Their children were sent to Ropery Walk School while others went to schools near to where they were now living such as Seaham High Colliery and Byron Terrace schools.

One of the Dorniers in this air raid was caught by a Beaufighter of 604 Squadron flown by Flying Officer Keele and Flying Officer Cowles based at Scorton. The Dornier crashed about thirty miles out to sea at 2.15 a.m. as it tried to make its way home to base. The body of the pilot, Unteroffizier Karl Roos (23), was given up by the sea on the beach at Blackhall Rocks and the body of Unteroffizier B. Mittelstadt was picked up from the sea. Other crew members, Obergefreiter G. Kaber and Unteroffizier A. Richter were not found. The Dornier U5-DP sank.

As the threat of invasion had now diminished, it was announced on Thursday 20 May that all road signposts were to be re-errected.

On Saturday 22 May there was a 'Wings' parade in Murton. This was part of the effort to raise £80,000 to buy four twin engined bombers for the R.A.F. and to start the 'Wings for Victory Week. Those taking part in the parade included the R.A.F., W.A.A.F., the A.T.C., Home Guard and Civil Defence Services.

The salute was taken in the Welfare Park by Squadron Leader T.S. Kitching who said in a speech afterwards, "In the coming battles of Europe we shall need air power on an even greater scale than we had in North Africa. When the time comes for use to break into Mr. Schicklegruber's so-called fortress of Europe, every aircraft we can put in the air will be playing a vital part in the combined effort. The lives of your husbands, fathers, sons and brothers will depend on the strength and extent of the air umbrella that we can keep up over the scene of operations."

The Home Guard gave a demonstration of a raiding party in the Welfare Park, for the benefit of 'Goopher birds' there was an exhibition of incendiary and high explosive bombs, pieces of ack-ack shells, remains of enemy flares and a collection of objects dropped from enemy planes.

Mrs. Sidney Webb, wife of the former M.P. for Seaham, had died this week and the news brought sadness to her many friends in the division. Sidney Webb was created a Labour Peer in 1929 as Lord Passfield but his wife, Beatrice Webb declined to assume the title preferring to remain known by the name she had always used as a writer and speaker. Mrs. Webb wrote many books on social and economic affairs and, with her husband, brought many speakers to Seaham including Lord Haldane and George Bernard Shaw. Mrs. Webb often wrote to the Women's Section of the Seaham Labour Party on political topics of the day.

Mr. Thomas J. Leighton married Miss Eleanor Lamb of Southwick last Saturday. Mr. Leighton was one of the prisoners rescued from the Altmark in a Norwegian fjord by the British destroyer, 'Cossack'. Mr.Leighton has since had other wartime adventures and was continuing with his seagoing calling.

A broadcast to occupied Czechoslovakia was given on Friday by a Czech national informing them that the British miners were their friends. The miners in Durham had collected £15,000 to rebuild Lidice when Czechoslovakia was finally liberated. The broadcast went on to say that the spirit of solidarity of the working people was just as important at this time.

Murton Women's Institute had set a target of £750 in their effort for 'Wings Week'. However, after only the first day of their campaign they had already raised £1,015.

On Friday 21 May Seaham Court heard of the non-attendance of five Home Guard men at their weekly parades. The five were fined £5 each. Also at the same court two men were fined for being absent from work. One of the men was said to have left his work saying that he was ill but it was known that he attended a dance that same evening.

In the very early hours of the morning of 24 May the air raid sirens were again wailing throughout the area and before long the sound of ack-ack gunfire could be heard. As every night, the seach-light batteries were sweeping the night sky trying to pick out the raiding bombers. In a while two magnesium parachute flares were seen over Murton as the bombers were looking to find their target. Six Firepot incendiary bombs fell on Murton Colliery pit heap at 3.15 a.m. three of which did not explode. Also, at Cold Heseldon, six Heavy Explosive bombs fell one of which did not explode. The N.E.E.S. Co.'s transformer house at Cold Heseldon received a direct hit and one man was injured in the incident.

In Dene Road, Dalton-le-Dale, the Hammond family had taken to their shared air-raid shelter. The occupants at this time were, Mr Bert Hammond and his wife Lydia, Bert's father Captain Hammond, Mrs Hammond's sister, Mrs. Swift, who was visiting from Sedburgh and who was also heavily pregnant, Mr. and Mrs. Foots and their son, John and Mr. Tulip who was the father of next door neighbour, Mrs. Seth

Some Optimism Begins to Surface

After some time the noise of gunfire and aircraft gradually lessened and all became quiet. Bert Hammond decided that, perhaps, this would be a good time to go back into his house and make a cup of tea for the group of tired people within the shelter. On going outside he took a look around to see that all was safe and well when he noticed a strange object lying across the top of the shelter. Blinking his eyes in disbelief he soon realised that this very large cigar shaped object was a parachute mine.

He then noticed that there was a parachute caught in a ten feet high Hawthorn tree next to the shelter. Stunned as he was he then realised that this mine might still explode. He returned inside the shelter and, calmly as he could, told the group of what he had found and that they all must leave. Wardens had seen the parachute mine descend into the village and soon located where it had landed. They ordered everyone in the area to vacate their homes and make their way to the Times Inn at the west end of the village. A messenger was sent ahead to inform the landlord of the inn what had happened and ask him to prepare to receive some of the refugees.

The group from the shelter and other neighbours gathered a few clothes and blankets and set off for the Times Inn. Some of the women were in tears by this time as they made their way to safety. As they neared St. Andrew's Church, Mr. Ivan Way, who was on fire watch duty, observed these shadowy figures moving along the village and thought at first were they perhaps paratrooper who had landed. Walking towards them he soon realised who they were and asked why and where they were going.

Mrs. Mary Wilson and her husband Tom had joined the group and Mary explained to Ivan what had happened. They had all been told to go to the Times Inn and await further instructions. They would not be allowed back to their homes for some time. An army truck arrived and five soldiers from the bomb disposal unit cordoned off the road and told the group to quickly make their way to the inn. One soldier stood guard while the others made off to Dene Road to make safe the land mine.

The group of refugees arrived at the Times Inn and were made comfortable in the large room which, from time to time, had been used as the venue for leek and vegetable shows. After about three hours, Mrs W. Thubron, who was the wife of the village butcher, arrived at the inn and invited those present to join her at her home for breakfast. Mr. and Mrs Thubron lived close by near St. Andrews Church.

Mrs. Swift, sister of Mrs. Hammond, had intended to stay with her sister in Dalton-le-Dale until after the birth of her baby so that she could be looked after by her sister. However, Mrs. Swift decided that she had better return to Sedbergh so, after having breakfast at the Thubron's home she caught an early bus back to Sedbergh. Still dressed in her night-dress but covered by a skirt and coat Mrs. Swift returned home and within a few days she gave birth to a lovely baby son.

The mine was made safe by early afternoon but was left in the village to be collected three days later. It had been made in Czechoslovakia and, but for the faulty clockwork mechanism of the detonator, would have caused a great loss of life and destruction. Given that other such parachute mines left craters almost forty feet wide by fifteen feet deep there is no doubt that those good people in the shelter had had a remarkable escape. About 10 per cent of these mines failed to explode; was this perhaps sabotage on the part of the Czechs.

Also at 3.05 a.m. a parachute mine exploded at Mount Pleasant, New Seaham and seriously damaged six houses and many other houses had slight damage. Huge lumps of clay were thrown out from the blast falling up to a hundred yards from the crater. A strange phenomenon occurred at Nichleson's baker's shop in Jubilee Avenue where the shop window was part sucked out of its frame and the window curtain came out of the side of the glass before the window slammed back into its frame. The glass did not break and is a fair example of the vacuum caused by such an explosion. A small boy was drowned in the water filled crater some time later and before the council could fill it up with ash waste.

These parachute mines had been used before as sea mines but were now used extensively as a land parachute mine or Luftmine. The mines dropped on Seaham were of 1,000 kilograms and were 8ft 8inches long and were dropped to earth, fairly gently so as not to damage the clockwork fuse mechanism, on blue-green artificial silk parachutes with a diameter of just under thirty feet. There were eighteen silk cords of about one and a half inches thick attaching the parachute to the mine. At the time of writing Mrs Seth still has a piece of the parachute cord from the mine that decended on the shelter in Dalton-le Dale.

The Durham Miners' Association which had already provided Spitfires and ambulances and also large sums of money to the Red Cross were now proposing to provide £2,500 as succour to prisoners of war. The object was to send 500 cigarettes or equivalent in tobacco to prisoners of war of each member or son or daughter of members of the Association who were in enemy hands. Each prisoner would also receive a quarterly supply of books up to the value of £1.

The past Vicar of Dawdon mentioned earlier was at this time confirmed as being safe and interned in Changi Camp, Singapore. Telegrams received at the Colonial Office through the Red Cross have shown his name included in a list of civilians now in the camp.

Seaham Squadron of the Air Training Corps paid another visit to their affiliated air base in Yorkshire on the weekend of 12 and 13 June. This was their third visit to the airfield. On their first visit in May the cadets numbered 100 and some of them were able to fly for the first time in service aircraft. During their second visit the squadron took part in the York 'Wings for Victory Week' parade. There was to be a week long visit to the station in the summer months with another short visit in the autumn.

Up to now there have been 60 members of the squadron who have gone into the services, most of them into the R.A.F. Several of these men were now serving in Rhodesia and Canada under the Empire Scheme.

Murton was without a barber in the middle of June. There were two resident barbers in Murton; one had not opened his shop in several weeks as he was at the time away from home. The other barber took a week off after having to work at high volume for many months.

Some Optimism Begins to Surface

The scouts camping ground at Shapley near Seaham was visited by Chief Scout, Lord Somers on Saturday 19 June. Lord Somers addressed a large gathering of scouts from all over the North East. The scout camp was gifted to the Scout movement about eight years earlier by George Gregson. There were 24 acres of field area, bush and woodland. There were twenty four camping sites of about an acre and at this particular meeting every one was taken up.

Four boys were up before the magistrates this week charged with wilful damage to air raid shelters. They were each fined 10s with 5s and though not a heavy fine the boys were made aware that this money would have to come from the hard earned pay of the father or mother.

At the end of the month Mr. J. E. Foreman of 18 Princess Road was asked if he would form the town's first 'Land Club'. Mr. Foreman was approached by Durham County War Agricultural Committee for his co-operation in this scheme as he had had wide experience in farming and was a keen gardener and allotment holder. The object of the Land Club was to provide farmers with assistance during harvest time. It was hoped that lists of willing workers would be drawn up so that they could be placed with farms when needed. The workers were to be paid at the usual rate for agricultural labourers.

The 4th July was designated 'Farm Sunday' in an effort to draw the general public's attention to the need for more volunteers to help with harvest work. There had been a bumper crop this year and Sir Frank Nicholson, Chairman of the County War Agricultural Committee, spoke to a large gathering in the grounds of the Houghall School of Agriculture, Durham. He described the harvest as 'a miracle' and showed the quality of farming in the country.

A committee was formed in Murton at the beginning of July to oversee the events for 'Holidays at Home' week starting on 24 July. Some of the events put forward for consideration included a beauty competition, a drum head service, women's cricket match, children's pet show, flower show, baby show and a fancy dress competition. There was also to be sports for the children, concerts and dramatic shows.

Mr. and Mrs Malcolm Dillon entertained a party of old age pensioners in the grounds of their home at Dene House on Saturday 3 July. There were recitations by Mrs Hannah Simpson (90) and Mrs Hurd, a younger pensioner. Another nonagenarian present at the garden party was Margaret Hannah Rogers. Both Mrs Simpson and Mrs Rogers lived in Emily Steet and had been friends since childhood. Both these old ladies could often be seen 'watching the world go by' on a seat near the Dawdon railway crossing.

'Farm Sunday', 4 July, saw a meeting at the School of Agriculture, Houghall arranged by the Ministry of Agriculture. It was emphasised by many speakers that there was still a great need for voluntary workers on farms over the coming weeks. There had been a magnificent effort by the agricultural community in producing the food but the harvest would be threatened if not enough people came forward to help gather in the harvest. The crops were expected to be the biggest harvest ever know in this country.

Chapter 5, 1943

Seaham First Aiders were given much praise on Tuesday 6 by Mr. W. Hewitson, Surgeon of Leeholm Hospital, Easington when he expressed great appreciation of the excellent work done by the First Aid personnel at Seaham. He said that the treatment of serious casualties indicated a very high standard of training and he had never seen a better treatment of serious casualties anywhere Mr. Hewitson's remarks were forwarded to Doctors Neilan, Black, Sacks and Weir who undertook first aid training at the first aid post, and also to the personnel of the Seaham Civil Defence casualty service.

First Class Stoker Stanley Hall R.N. was returned to his home in Seaham from an Italian prisoner of war camp, Sulmona in Italy. He had been serving in a submarine which was sunk in August 1940. He was taken prisoner along with 48 other men. A number of these men were repatriated this week in exchange for Italian prisoners in this country. In the camp at Sulmona the prisoners had one meal a day which was a kind of thin stew and meat was added once a week. There were about 3000 prisoners in the camp and they found that the Red Cross parcels and the parcels from home helped to make up their daily food intake. Mr. Hall described the attitude of the Italian guards as friendly.

Mr. John McCutcheon reporting at the Parks and General Purposes Committee said that the number of allotments in Seaham now stood at 875. Of these 390 were pr-war 485 wartime. The British Restaurant had been supplied with produce to the value of £5 14s 7d during the past quarter.

A new system of air raid warnings was about to be introduced in order to give a quicker warning of approaching enemy aircraft. The normal siren would be sounded but information of attack was expected to be much more efficient. Mr. Herbert Morrison M.P. said that a reorganisation of Observer Centres carried out by the Air Ministry found a number of ways to improve the process of getting the information out to the districts.

There was a garden party held in the vicarage grounds on Saturday 17 July where there was music, entertainment and games and also a white elephant stall. All the proceeds were for the bazaar fund.

In the Drill Hall that evening, the A.T.C. staged a boxing tournament. There were sixteen contests arranged between boys from the A.T.C. and other boys clubs as well as men from the Home Guard and Civil Defence.

In the middle of July, miners in the area were being asked if they could write short talks in French or have them translated into French. The B.B.C. was asking for such items that they could broadcast in their weekly Trade Union programme which they broadcast to the French mining community. The wife of one miner broadcast a talk in French on 'Wartime Conditions in the Durham Coalfield.'

An Easington school master was on his way to entertain troops at their camp at Seaham Hall on Monday night 19 July. Mr. Pat Terry, an accomplished ventriloquist was taking his 'pals', Joe Higgins and Alice Goodchild to the show and his 'pals' were resting in a suitcase in the back of his car. However, when Pat arrived at the camp the suitcase was gone and the performance had to be cancelled. This unlikely couple were 'absent without leave' for nine days before they were returned in good condition to Mr.Terry so the entertainment of the troops in the area could continue.

A salvage 'Book Drive' got underway on 24 July until 7 August and the aim was for two books per head of the population which was thought would bring in 40,000 books. Some of the books would go to those serving in the forces and others would go to libraries which had been damaged in air raids. Those books suitable for children would go to children's hospitals and any others that were not wanted would be sent to be re-pulped.

Again there was no Durham Miner's Gala this year and the last one was in July 1939. Then there were Sword Dancers in North Road entertaining the crowds, Cullercoats fishwives selling their wares to the throng of people on Station Bank. The race course was filled to capacity with families having their annual picknick. Now all was quiet but perhaps it would not be to long before 'The Big Meeting' would again bring colour back to the streets of old Durham City.

In the first week of August a telegram arrived at the home of Mrs Dobson of Victoria Terrace, Murton reporting that her son, Flying Officer Rober E. Dobson had failed to return to base after an operational flight. However, the telegram stated that the crew were safe and in neutral territory. Robert had only just married Miss Kitty Lightfoot one month before this. He was well know as a cricketer before the war.

Two young 'blue jackets' were fined this week for being drunk and disorderly in Dawdon. One of the men was from Seaham and the other from Sunderland.

The new British Restaurant at Deneside was opened on Monday 2 August and wholesome meals were provided at the cost of 10d; - soup 2d, meat and vegetables 6d and a sweet for 2d. This restaurant would be open every day, except Sunday, between the hours of 11.30 a.m. and 1.30 p.m.

Although there had been a call for farm workers one labour camp in County Durham had some problems. The campers there had been at the camp for five days and had not yet been given any farm work at all. They were expected to be in the camp for one month and although they had been guaranteed work the campers were finding it hard just sitting around.

A concert was held in Church Street Methodists Church on the evening of 25 August with one of Britain's leading sopranos taking part. She was Miss Isobel Baillie who was well known because of her many B.B.C broadcasts. The programme also featured Mr. Jack Wick (tenor) and Mr. W.T. Leighton (bass). The choir was made up of all the free churches in the circuit.

A brother and sister were able to meet up in the Middle East this month. Mr. Edward Moses, a Chief Officer in a large British ship met with his sister, Miss Edna Moses, who is a Queen Alexandra Imperial Military Nursing Sister serving in the Middle East. Mr. Moses was given a few days leave in order to spend some time with his sister sightseeing.

Chapter 5, 1943

The Medical Officer for Seaham, Dr. J.W. Peden, gave his report for 1942 on the Seaham Health Department of Seaham Urban Council. Statistics showed a birth ratio of 18.1 per 1,000 of the population and the figure for England and Wales was 15.1 per 1,000. From July 1942 there had been 287 cases of scabies 233 had been cleared. However, Diphtheria was still a big problem and were mostly cases of children between the ages of 5 and 15 years old. 50 had been removed to hospital and 83% of those cases had not been immunised. Seven deaths had occurred and none of these patients had been immunised.

The Reverent John Bell, a well known Murton Methodist Minister and who was serving as a padre in India had a chance meeting with a Murton man in a cinema in Darjeeling. This Himalayan station was one he visited while on leave from the city and when he attended the film show he struck up in conversation with a Flight Sergeant Pilot who was sitting next to him. It turned out that the pilot was Bazil Skeen, a former employee at Murton Colliery Offices.

The following Sunday Ft. Sgt. Skeen took his friends along to the local Church of Scotland to hear the Reverend Bell preach. They all rounded off their meeting with a party in one of Darjeeling's quaint cafe's.

Keen gardening paid off for a Seaham man on Saturday 28 August at the Great Yorkshire Show held in Bradford. Mr. Adam Reed of 11 Alfred Steet, Seaham had entered a truss of 'Stoner's Exhibition' tomatoes and had won the first prize of £25. He was long known for the quality of his produce in local shows where he exhibited both flowers and vegetables.

At a meeting of Dalton-le-Dale Women's Institute on Friday 3 September, presided over by Mrs. E. Vout, it was arranged to have a collection for the Children's Hospital in Sunderland. Mrs. Collings spoke on 'Household Hints to Remember'. There was also an exhibition of vegetables and the winners were Mrs. Mullen, Mrs. Smith and Mrs. Finlay. All of the garden produce was later sent to the Sunderland Royal Infirmary.

Seaham and District Allotment Society gave a donation of £5 to a fund opened by the National Allotment Society. This fund was to supply seeds and equipment to people of enemy occupied countries as soon as they were liberated. The aim was to help these people to resume a normal life again and to provide food for themselves again.

The Seaham Church Lads' Brigade had returned from camp at Hurworth this week and all the boys had had a wonderful time together. The camp by the river made an excellent base and the campers spent a great deal of time swimming. Food and finances were provided by the boy's parents and the event was such a success that next years camp was already being discussed.

News came this week of a missing soldier, Bombardier F. Keegan R.A. of 24 Hawthorn Square, Seaham. He had been reported missing in Malaya but a post card arrived at his home this week informing relatives that he was now a prisoner of war in 'Japanese hands.'

Forms were now available to apply to buy 'Utility' furniture. The forms were available at local Fuel Offices. Permits to buy 15 square yards of rationed curtain material could be obtained by applicants who comply with regulations regarding utility furniture.

After the recent 'Book Drive' a number of interesting books came to light. One of these was a 69 year old publication, a F. White & Co. Directory of 1847. This general directory of places like Newcastle, Sunderland and Durham had items on towns such as Seaham. Two pages were devoted to Seaham and tell of an omnibus which 'leaves from the Golden Lion at 4 p.m. daily. The visiting doctor to Seaham Infirmary was Dr. W.R. Clanny of Sunderland. Dr. Clanny was a founder of the research to find a successful safety lamp for miners. At this time there were public baths at the north end of the town run by Mr. William Fairless who was also the keeper of the lighthouse.

Further word was received from the Archdeacon Graham White who, with his wife, is a prisoner of war in Changi Camp, Singapore. The letter said, 'We are both well, no more can be said except adieu.' He sent good wishes to all friends in Seaham.

On Sunday afternoon 19 September Seaham Harbour St. Mary Magdalen's Drama Society presented four one act plays for the patients at Seaham Hall Sanatorium. The plays were, 'Musical Burlesque', 'The Old Aged Pensioner', 'Three Wishes' and 'A Boy in Uniform' The patients, mostly young women, were richly entertained giving them the chance to forget their worries for a few hours.

Youngsters were again showing what they could do for the war effort at this time. Four little girls put on a concert and a 'bring and buy' sale to raise money for 'Mrs Churchill's Aid to Russia Fund.' These children, Brenda Compton (8), Jaqueline Gentles (11), Muriel Curry (11) and Mary Watts (10) raised £10 10s and sent a cheque for this amount to Mrs. Churchill together with the following letter:

'Dear Mrs. Churchill,

With the aim of helping your Aid to Russia Fund, we four friends arranged a 'bring and buy' sale last week and with a small concert have been able to raise £10 10s and a cheque is enclosed for this amount, which I hope you will accept with our best wishes. We hope you enjoyed your journey to Canada.'

At the end of September a photograph of a group of prisoners of war arrived in Murton. Among those in the group was Telegraphist J. N. Wilson R.N. of 12 Pilgrim Street, Murton. Some of the other men in the picture were from County Durham. The men all looked to be in good spirits.

Early in October, Rowntree's issued the Personal Points Values for chocolate on 'the ration.' 4 Points for their Fine Chocolate, 2 Points for Blended, 2 Points for Chocolate Cream Tablets, 2 Points for Chocolate Assorted Centres. In order to save on packaging the company was now selling Rowntrees Gums loose at 7d per quarter pound.

Mr Jack Wick gave a fine musical evening in Church Street Methodists Hall on Saturday evening 30 October. Mr Wick was accompanied by other entertainers and Miss J. A..Farrow, Head Mistress of Seaham Secondary School for Girls took her place as Chairman for the evening. Also on this day, Seaham Wagon Works Field Permanent Allotment Association held a Chrysanthemum show in the Dawdon Hotel. The display was also open to view on Sunday. Gifts of flowers were sold in aid of Red Cross funds.

At the beginning of November Seaham Food Committee decided to once more tackle the Ministry of Food about the shortage of fish and fruit in Seaham. Some Ministry Officials were reluctant to believe this was the case but there was evidence to support the Food Committee's claim.

Seaham Urban Council asked the Surveyor to report on property in the Dawdon and New Seaham area that might be suitable for 'cash and carry' restaurants. This was prompted by the success of the British Restaurant in Adelaide Row, Seaham.

On Wednesday 10 November 80 cadets of the Seaham Squadron A.T.C. were given the whole day to use an aircraft at a Royal Air Force station in the North East. The lads spent the day flying and learning about the aircraft. This was a real hands-on experience that was enjoyed by the Squadron.

At the beginning of the month, Mr. Lawrence Whitwell, of 30 Strangeways Street, Dawdon was elected as a member of Durham County Council for the Seaham No. 3 Division. Mr. Whitwell was Assistant Check Weighman at Dawdon Colliery and a member of Dawdon Miner's Lodge. He came to Dawdon from Kelloe in 1910. He was greatly interested in the St. John's Ambulance Association and was a holder of the Voucher, Certificate and Medallion of the Association as well as the Gold Medal for being the best student of the Dawdon Ambulance Class of 1929.

In the second week of November, Private Thomas Coulson (33), who had been a prisoner of war since his capture in Norway three and a half years earlier was repatriated to his home in Bethune Avenue, Seaham. On Saturday 13 he was presented with a gift as did Corporal Fred Elliot at the Dawdon Chrysanthemum Show. On the Sunday he was entertained by his friends at the British Legion Club where he received another gift.

At the end of the month Seaham Library discovered a map of County Durham of 1825. At that time Seaham consisted of the small hamlet around Seaham Hall or Seaham House as it was then called. The tower in Dawdon Dene is referred to as 'Daden Tower.' This is very similar to the vernacular use of the word Dalden.

Seaham Divisional Labour Party convened a meeting in early December in the Thornley Miner's Welfare Hall in which Mr Shinwell spoke on what we should be looking to when the war was over. Mr. Shinwell was concerned at some negative feelings that were surfacing. "It is careless and dangerous to suggest that Britain will be a poor country after the war. This is not the way to encourage the men who are fighting our battles. To tell them that after their struggles and sacrifices they will return to poverty is poor consolation and is calculated to weaken moral and lower Great Britain in the eyes of other nations. I have only one concern and I am sure that it is shared by millions of other people that is to uphold the prestige of the country, to uphold the standard of living for everybody and to set a fine example for every other nation to follow."

In the second week of December a man in Seaham received three tax demands on his property, all from the same office, all addressed to him in three different envelopes and all posted at the same time. In each was enclosed a 'War Economy Label' for re-use of the envelopes in order to save paper. It seems that nothing much changes.

There was also a complaint from Easington Food Control Committee that some shopkeepers in Seaham were selling sweets towards the end of the ration period against coupons relating to the succeeding ration period. It was pointed out that this was an offence on the part of the retailer and the purchaser. This was seen as unfair to others and action would be taken against those involved.

By the middle of December the area was hit by an influenza epidemic. Miners were issued with anti-influenza tablets and many children missed school because of the illness.

Lord Lonndonderry was opening a bazaar in the Church Hall, Seaham, on Saturday 18 December presided over by Miss N. Dillon. She expressed regret that her father, Mr Malcolm Dillon, could not officiate as he had the 'flue. In declaring the bazaar open, Lord Londonderry said that he was deputising for Lady Londonderry who was suffering the same complaint

Speaking of Mr Churchill who had been ill over the past few weeks, the Marquis said, "He is imbued with the British spirit which never knows defeat and he is determined to fight the battle to the very end. He has helped us greatly by his speeches and broadcasts and we all owe him a deep debt of gratitude for the splendid service he has rendered to the Nation."

Two cousins from Seaham met in the Middle East whilst serving in the forces. William Newton Fox who lived with his parents at 33 Longnewton Street, Dawdon and who was in the Royal Corps of Signals for nine years, met up with his cousin, William Douglas Baxter whose parents live at the Times Inn, Dalton-le-Dale. Mr Baxter had been in the Royal Air Force for three years and had been overseas for eighteen months.

The Seaham Area Committee of the Durham County Drama Association put on a series of one act plays in the Spiritual Hall on Thursday 16 December. 'I Made it Possible' by Seaham Townswomen's Guild, 'The Dear Departed' by Mrs F.L. Armstrong and company, 'A Dust-Up at Madames' by Seaham and Dawdon Townswomen's Guild and excerpt from 'The Merry Wives of Windsor' were the four plays enjoyed by a full house. The proceeds went to the Red Cross Fund.

The fifth wartime Christmas arrived and the austerity measures were as tight as ever. The people of the town went about their usual spiritual Christmas celebrations and made merry as best they could. It had been a difficult year at home but prospects abroad were showing signs of success and there was real hope that the end of the war would not be to far off. The air raid warning sirens still occasionally wailed throughout the night but people were well used to the disruption to their lives and by getting on with life showed little regard for such inconvenience.

The Golden Wedding of Robert Wilkinson Carr and his wife was celebrated on 30 December. Mr. Carr had worked in the mines for 62 years and at the age of 72 was still at work. He arrived at Dawdon Colliery from Chester Moor Colliery 36 years earlier. He had met and married his wife at Chester Moor on December 30 1893. Mr. Carr was now working underground at Dawdon greasing rollers on the main haulage way.

King's Message To The Empire

"With God's Help, We Shall Prevail"

FROM his study in Buckingham Palace on Sunday night His Majesty the King broadcast a message to the people of the Empire. He wore the dark blue undress uniform of an Admiral of the Fleet. The King was alone in the study, and Her Majesty listened to the speech from another room in the Palace. This message is to be sent to every householder in the country:—

In this grave hour, perhaps the most fateful in our history, I send to every household of my people, both at home and overseas, this message spoken with the same depth of feeling for each one of you as if I were able to cross your threshold and speak to you myself.

For the second time in the lives of most of us we are at war. Over and over again we have tried to find a peaceful way out of the differences between ourselves and those who are now our enemies. But it has been in vain. We have been forced into a conflict. For we are called with our Allies to meet the challenge of a principle which, if it were to prevail, would be fatal to any civilised order in the world.

It is the principle which permits a State in the selfish pursuit of power to disregard its treaties and its solemn pledges which sanctions the use of force or threat of force against the sovereignty and independence of other States. Such a principle stripped of all disguise is surely the more primitive doctrine that might is right, and if this principle were established throughout the world the freedom of our own country and of the whole British Commonwealth of Nations would be in danger.

But far more than this—the peoples of the world would be kept in the bondage of fear and all hopes of settled peace and of the security of justice and liberty among nations would be ended. This is the ultimate issue which confronts us. For the sake of all that we ourselves hold dear and of the world's order and peace it is unthinkable that we should refuse to meet the challenge.

It is to this high purpose that I now call my people at home and my peoples across the seas who will make our cause their own. I ask them to stand calm and firm and united in this time of trial.

The task will be hard. There may be dark days ahead and war can no longer be confined to the battlefield; but we can only do the right as we see the right and reverently commit our cause to God. If, one and all, we keep resolutely faithful to it, ready for whatever service or sacrifice it may demand, then, with God's help, we shall prevail. May He bless and keep us all.

1. A message from the King.

BEFORE, DURING AND AFTER THE RAID

FITTING BEDS IN YOUR ANDERSON SHELTER

—and the help that is ready if your home is hit

WITH very little trouble you can make your Anderson steel shelter a comfortable sleeping place for your family. Four adults and four babies, for example, or four adults and two older children can sleep in a standard Anderson shelter, 6 ft. 6 ins. in length.

All the tools you need are hammer, saw, and pliers that will cut wire. The materials are a few feet of timber, not less than 1½" square, some nails, and some canvas (or hessian, burlap, stout wire netting or similar material).

QUITE AN EASY JOB

Look at the diagram of the arrangement of bunks and you will at once see the idea. The top bunks run from one end of the shelter to the other, the ends resting on the angle-irons that run across the shelter at each end. These bunks should be 20 inches wide, and about 6 ft. 6 ins. long. The lower bunks are the same size, but rest on the floor, on legs 4 ins. high.

THE CHILDREN'S BUNKS

The cross bunks for the children are about 4 ft. 6 ins. long, and have four legs each 14 ins. high, which rest on the side pieces of the upper and lower bunks. The cross bunks can be up to 2 ft. wide. The legs must be nailed on inside the shelter. Fix canvas, hessian, etc., across the bunks and the job is finished.

These hints are taken from a very helpful leaflet which is being issued by local authorities to all who have Anderson shelters.

SEE THOSE FRIENDS TODAY

. . . and make plans to go and stay with them, or for *them* to come and stay with *you*, if either of your houses is knocked out.

Help is ready
If you can't make your own arrangements and you have to leave your home go to a Rest Centre. Ask your warden where one is. There you will get food and clothes and somewhere to sleep. You will be given advice on your problems and help in finding a new home.

If your gas is cut off
There may be a communal feeding centre nearby, where you can get hot meals at very low prices. Find out about it, and if there isn't one, fix up to eat with friends or relations.

ISSUED BY THE MINISTRY OF HOME SECURITY

2. Sleeping in the Anderson shelter.

MINISTRY OF FOOD

REASONS FOR RATIONING

War has meant the re-planning of our food supplies. Half our meat and most of our bacon, butter and sugar come from overseas. Here are four reasons for rationing:—

① RATIONING PREVENTS WASTE OF FOOD We must not ask our sailors to bring us unnecessary food cargoes at the risk of their lives.

② RATIONING INCREASES OUR WAR EFFORT Our shipping carries food, and armaments in their raw and finished state, and other essential raw materials for home consumption and the export trade. To reduce our purchases of food abroad is to release ships for bringing us other imports. So we shall strengthen our war effort.

③ RATIONING DIVIDES SUPPLIES EQUALLY There will be ample supplies for our 44½ million people, but we must divide them fairly, everyone being treated alike. No one must be left out.

④ RATIONING PREVENTS UNCERTAINTY Your Ration Book assures you of your fair share. Rationing means that there will be no uncertainty—*and no queues.*

YOUR RATION BOOK IS YOUR PASSPORT TO EASY PURCHASING OF BACON & HAM, BUTTER AND SUGAR

AN ANNOUNCEMENT BY THE MINISTRY OF FOOD, GT. WESTMINSTER HOUSE, LONDON, S.W.1

3. Reasons for rationing.

Hints on WAR-TIME SPENDING AND SAVING

Here are three ships

1 This one is loaded with foodstuffs and necessaries

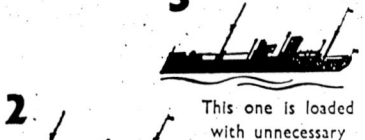

2 This one is loaded with munitions

3 This one is loaded with unnecessary goods

By limiting your purchases of the goods contained in Ship No. 3, you leave more cargo space for the goods we need to win the war. Spend carefully then—buy what you must—but avoid spending on unnecessary things, particularly goods which come from abroad.

Result:

(1) You increase the shipping available for essentials.

(2) You have more money to invest in National Savings Certificates and the New Defence Bonds.

HOW TO LEND TO HELP WIN THE WAR

1. National Savings Certificates
Free of Income Tax. Price 15s. Value after 5 years 17s. 6d. After 10 years 20s. 6d., which equals interest at £3 3s. 5d. per cent. Maximum holding 500 Certificates including earlier issues.

2. 3% Defence Bonds
£5 and multiples of £5. Income Tax NOT deducted at source. Maximum holding £1,000.

3. Post Office Savings Bank and Trustee Savings Banks.
Any sum from 1s. upwards with annual limit of £500.

★ To Employers and Employees
Has a National Savings Group been formed in your office, works or shop? If not, write at once to the National Savings Committee, London, S.W.1. Savings Groups provide the best and easiest method of accumulating weekly savings.

Lend to defend the right to be free

ISSUED BY THE NATIONAL SAVINGS COMMITTEE

4. Wartime spending and saving.

5. The author's school photograph, 1940.

6. Seaham Auxiliary Fire Service, 1940.

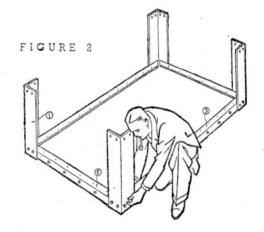

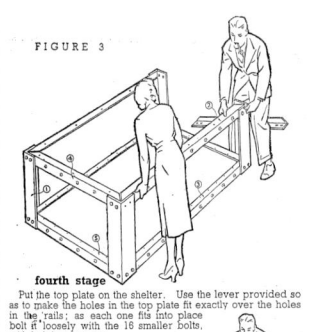

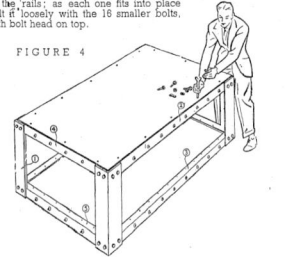

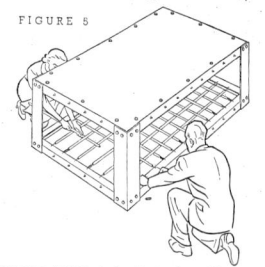

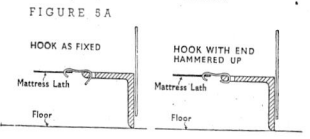

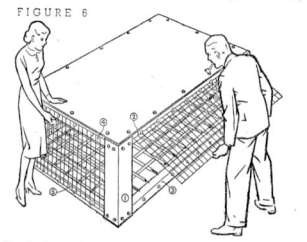

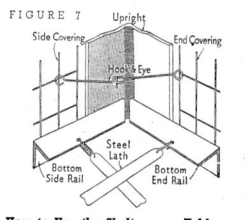

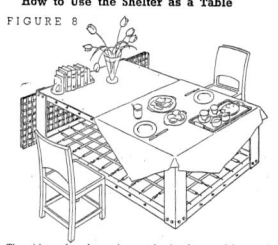

7. *Setting up a Morrison shelter.*

8. *Canadian Tim Sheedy and his wife Mary.*

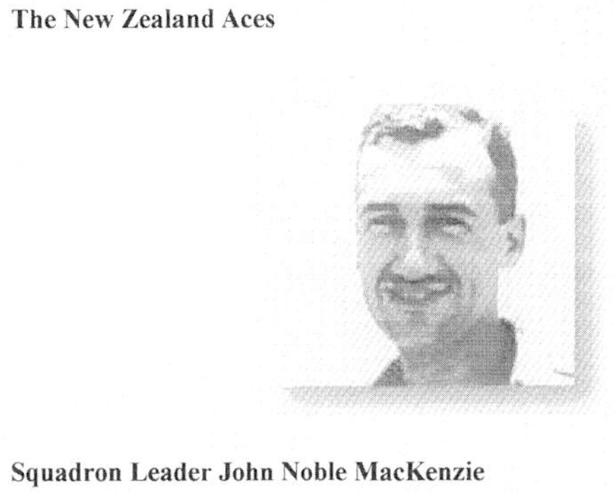

The New Zealand Aces

Squadron Leader John Noble MacKenzie

9. *Squadron Leader J. N. McKenzie D.F.C.*    10. *An Army Christmas card from North Africa.*

11. *H.M.S. Seaham on sea trials off Stornoway.*

12. A parachute mine similar to that which landed on the Hammond's shelter.

13. *School children with H.M.S. Seaham cup, 1944.*

14. The headstone of P.O. J. F. Dowding.

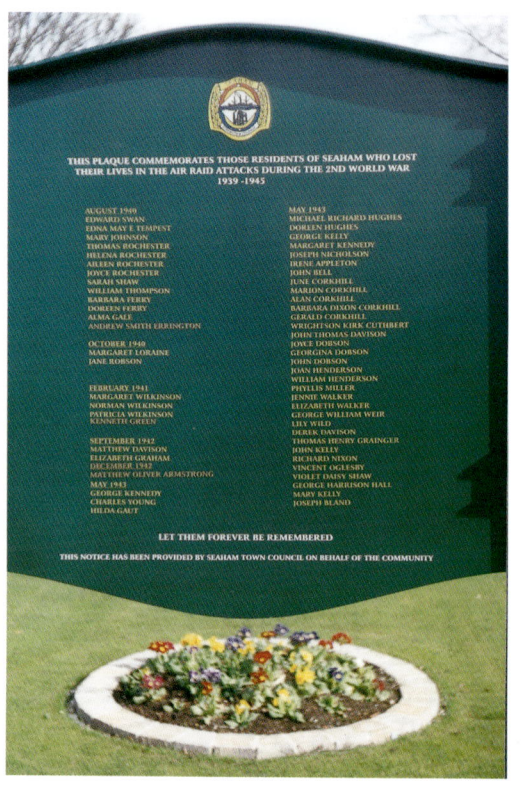

15. Commemorative plaque to civilians who died in air raids.

16. Army 'pill box' near the Times Inn, 2002

17. The war ends - The author aged 12 (right) cheering the Prime Minister.

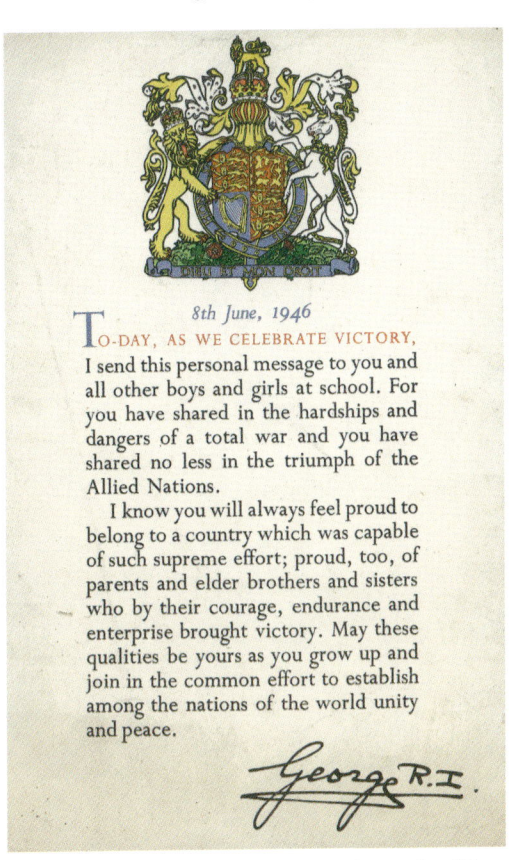

8th June, 1946

TO-DAY, AS WE CELEBRATE VICTORY, I send this personal message to you and all other boys and girls at school. For you have shared in the hardships and dangers of a total war and you have shared no less in the triumph of the Allied Nations.

I know you will always feel proud to belong to a country which was capable of such supreme effort; proud, too, of parents and elder brothers and sisters who by their courage, endurance and enterprise brought victory. May these qualities be yours as you grow up and join in the common effort to establish among the nations of the world unity and peace.

George R.I.

18. A message to all children from the King.

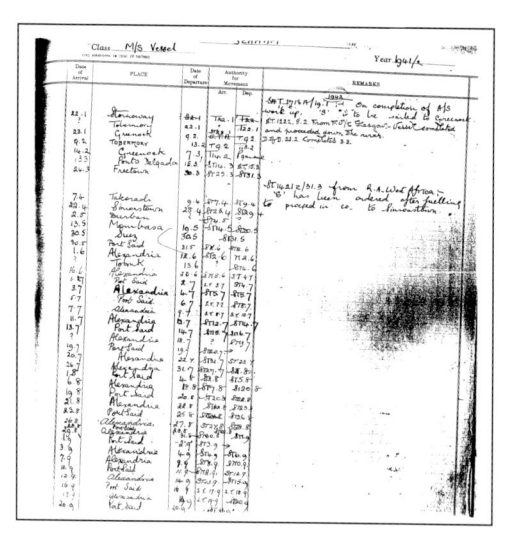

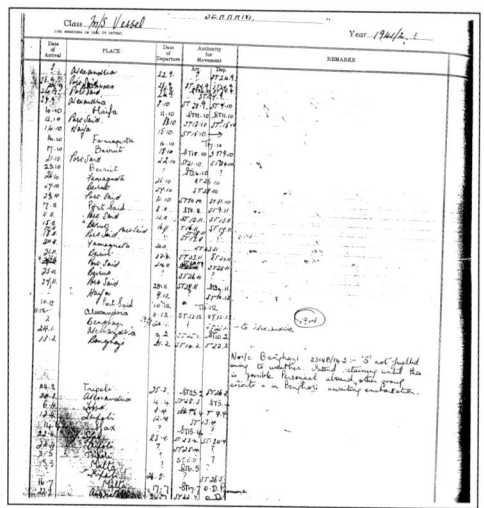

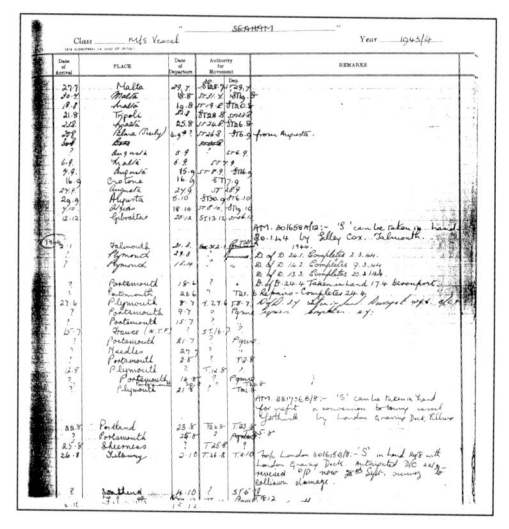

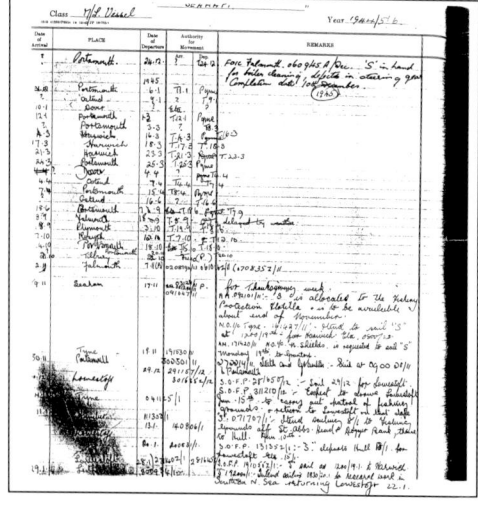

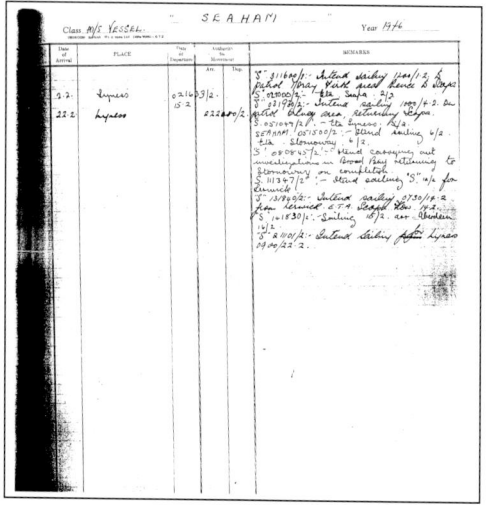

19. From the ship's log, H.M.S. Seaham 1941 - 1946.

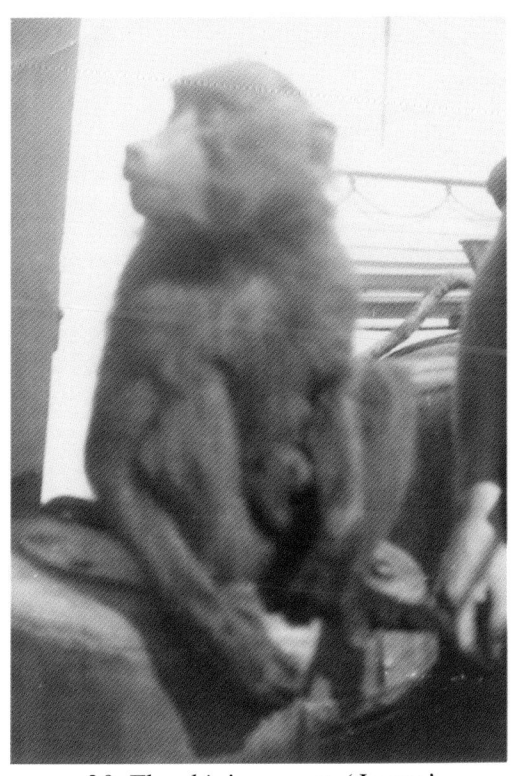

20. The ship's mascot, 'Jenny.'

21. Joe Bragger in Alexandria, 1942.

22. Italian submarine, 'Bronzo' being towed by H.M.S. Seaham.

23. Survivors from 'Bronzo' on board H.M.S. Seaham.

24. Identity papers of Rodolfo Borrani of the submarine 'Bronzo.'

25. Lt. Commander Brett with 2nd i/c of the Italian submarine.

26. L to R - 1st Lieut. W.S. Dawson, Lieut. C.H. Sharpe and Seaman C. Mooney.

27. *Children of West Lea Junior School with H.M.S. Seaham cup 1994.*

Chapter 6, 1944

'And Miles to go Before I Sleep'

There were two New Years Honours awarded in Seaham this year. An M.B.E. was awarded to Mrs. Thomasina Todd for her work with women and children in the area as well as for her Seaham Urban District Council duties and also for her work as a magistrate.

The other award was the B.E.M. awarded to Mr. William Shotton of Exeter Avenue, Deneside, a member of the Seaham Rescue Service, for the gallantry he displayed in the rescue of a boy and a young woman in an extremely dangerous position after bombing by enemy action.

The rescue party had had to tunnel for thirteen hours through 12 feet of debris including timber and through layers of 14 inch thick brick wall. In time a tunnel was made and a doctor was able to administer morphine to the young woman who was trapped by her feet. The rescued boy was seven years old George Corkhill the only survivor of a family of six. He had already lost a father, mother, two sisters and a brother in an air raid. The young woman, Mary Kelly, aged nineteen unfortunately died in hospital.

There had been two or three cases at Seaham Court where boys had been sent to Approved Schools. However, it was found that there were no places left for these boys . The schools, reformative in character, were seen as the best way of teaching these boys of the errors of their ways but if these schools were full then other measures would have to be taken. The problem of juvenile crime was one of the difficult problems of the time and answers to the problem needed to be found.

Because of the losses still taking place at Seaham British Restaurant with regard to cutlery, it was suggested that people should be asked to take their own when they visited the restaurant. However, the Council did not want the public to feel that there was no adequate provision of cutlery. It was finally agreed that it would be a good idea to appoint an elderly person who could supervise the issue of cutlery. It was felt that it was mainly children who were making of with the cutlery and not the regular adult customers.

A complimentary benefit concert was given by friends of Mr. Robert Young of Park Street, Seaham, on Wednesday evening 26 January in the Church Street Methodist Church. Mr. Young was one of the best known musicians in the area and had played the violin for over 60 years. At the age of eleven he had performed in 'The Messiah' at Haswell where he then lived.

Chapter 6, 1944

At the concert there were a number of well known artists including some personal friends of Mr. Young. Among the entertainers were Madam S. Bailes (soprano), Madam Emerson (contralto), Mr. Jack Wick (tenor) and Mr. T. Leighton (bass).

Seaham Branch of the Durham County Library was holding an exhibition of drawings this week by amateur artist Mr. Robert Firth of 8 Ambleside Avenue, Seaham, who is employed at Vane Tempest Colliery. The drawings were portraits of film stars including Ginger Rogers, Merle Oberon, Claudette Colbert, Jessie Matthews, Leslie Howard, Conrad Veidt and Spencer Tracy.

The famous Barnado Musical Boys from London visited Dawdon Miners Hall on Saturday 5 February and were warmly welcomed by the audience. Counc. S. Barratt presided and an address was given by Counc. the Reverend H. Entwhistle. The boys were supported in this concert by local artists.

Durham County Council's Agricultural Education Committee offered film displays to Seaham Urban Council together with demonstrations in an effort to encourage the 'Dig for Victory Campaign.' The Seaham Council gratefully accepted the offer.

In the first week of February, the Seaham Urban District Council decided that the case for 'star' lighting in the town should remain in abeyance. There was no chance of getting the materials and labour to do this work for several months and whether the work could go ahead next winter would probably depend on the opening of the 'Second Front.'

Windows that had been damaged in St. John's Parish Church through enemy action were now replaced but not with the beautiful stained glass as before but with ordinary clear glass. The east window was badly damaged in the raid and the nave window had contained the armorial bearings of Vane Stewart, Tempest, McDonnell and others interwoven with the Marquis of Londonderry.

A woman out shopping in Church Street this week lost two £1 notes and when she arrive home she waited until her husband came home from work before reporting the loss to the police. With great surprise the couple were told that the money had been handed in within a few minutes of the woman losing the notes. A sign that there were still honest people to be found in the town after the bad publicity of the missing cutlery at the British Restaurant.

'Red Riding Hood' was this year pantomime given by the Seaham Amateur Operatic Society and the production started on 7 February in the Theatre Royal and played for five nights to packed houses. The Producer was Mr. Jack Hilton of South Shields and the original music was written by the Musical Director, Mr. Stan Hunter of Seaham. The scenery was specially painted by Mr. George Toft.

Because of a lessening of night air raids work was now going on to introduce 'modified lighting' in the Seaham area though the electrical engineer said that it would be something like three months before fittings would be delivered and thereafter it would be well into the summer before anything could be done. Modified lighting would be a step in the right direction but would not be available until the autumn of 1944. The full street lighting would still be a very long way off.

Mr. Harold Cattermole (21) son of Mr and Mrs Cattermole of 14 Ross Street, Seaham, this month gained his wings in the R.A.F. Harold, a former butcher's assistant was trained to fly in South Africa after joining the R.A.F. in 1942.

Seaham Highways Committee was now pressing the Ministry of Transport to permit the removal of road barriers in the town. These concrete road blocks such as the on at the west end of The Avenue at Mount Pleasant and also the one at the west end of Castlereagh Road were considered a hazard to road traffic and were now thought to be unnecessary as an enemy invasion was now not considered to be likely.

As gas masks had been issued four or five years earlier a warning was given that they should be examined for damage. Repair was available or replacement would be given free of charge throughout January and February, 1944.

Flight Sergeant J. Scollan (22) of Seaham has written that he is now engaging the enemy as a night fighter pilot in the R.A.F. serving in Italy. Ft. Sgt. Scollan had served in merchant ships and was involved as a gunner. While serving on an oil tanker bound for the West Indies, the ship was sunk while being escorted to the convoy by a pilot boat. All the crew were taken off by the pilot boat. Ft.Sgt. Scollan gave up the sea and enlisted in the Royal Air Force and he joined his night fighter squadron in July, 1942.

There was some concern about rumours that Mr. Emanuel Shinwell M.P. might be in line for the shipping post in Washington under the Ministry of War Transport, a post vacated recently by Sir Arthur Salter. However, on Saturday 5 February Mr. Shinwell was visiting his Seaham constituency and he killed the rumour when he said that he would never accept a post which would prevent him from keeping that close touch with his constituents which he had maintained over the past eight years.

East Durham Brewster Sessions revealed that in Seaham there were 18 convictions for drunkenness in 1943. This was an increase of six over the figure for 1942, out of a population of 20,000. Castle Eden had 82 convictions an increase of twelve out of a 7,300 population. Was, perhaps, Nimo's Best Bitter the underlying reason for drunkenness in Castle Eden?

It was at this time that the issue of bus shelters was raised in a report by Mr J. W. Gray, Clerk to Easington Rural Council. The Minister of War Transport had suggested co-operation with the bus operating companies and had given promises of support for materials for the erection of bus shelters in the area. This support would only be for the erection of bus shelters in the most essential places.

Saturday 25 February saw three coal mines on strike with 5,000 men taking part. The mines affected were Dawdon, Seaham and Elmore Collieries. The strikes were caused by the men being dissatisfied with the Porter Awards. A return to work was affected by Sunday but both Seaham and Dawdon Miner's Lodges asked Durham Miner's Association to call a special meeting at an early date so that delegates could express their views and dissatisfaction over the anomalies in the Porter Award with reference to piece work and in particular to putters under 21 years old.

At a meeting of the Seaham Divisional Labour Party on 25 February Mr. Shinwell M.P. spoke about the criticism he had levelled at the government over recent months. The reconstruction programme was not going well and there had been to many delays in reaching decisions. Mr. Shinwell did not blame the Prime Minister for this, indeed he said that the P.M. had enough to occupy his mind at the moment. Lord Woolton, Minister for Reconstruction, had been doing a lot of talking he said and some of what he said he liked very much but that did not mean he could just go on talking. Lord Woolton must act with speed or otherwise the good reputation that he had gained as Minister for Food would vanish into thin air.

The Miner's Training Centre at Horden took in 90 trainees on Monday 27 February and this was the second time this figure had been reached. Eighty men left the previous week to take up posts at various collieries and since the start of the scheme about 500 men received preliminary training.

Seaham Squadron of the Air Training Corps hosted the boxing championships between the North East and North West Commands on Saturday 19 March. This event was very prestigious and was largely due to the organisational skills of Flight Lieutenant J. C. Jennings and the encouragement of his officers that the championship was being held at Seaham.

One of the boys taking part in the contest had wanted to stay at home because his father was ill. However, his father told him he must attend , "The game counts; go and win your contest." The cadet was J. Hand Dearne who, in one of the best fights of the evening, went on to win.

Among the 'Top Brass' present were Sir Bertram Jones, Financial Advisor to the Air Ministry, Air Commodore S. W. Smith, Commander North East Command and Major W. J. Taylor, Chairman of Yorkshire A.T.C. Association. The event was attended by almost 1,000 sports fans.

The debate on the Nationalisation of the coal industry was now in full swing and Mr. Will Lawther, President of the National Minworkers Federation of Great Britain, said that it would win the complete confidence of miners and their families. He said that the industry could not be run efficiently and get the best out of it if very miner loathed his industry because of its owners.

Fifth Form girls at the Seaham Girl's Grammar School performed the play, 'As You Like It' on Wednesday 29 March to the delight of a large appreciative audience. Also on Wednesday evening there were plays produced in Rock House by the Girls Training Corps, St. Mary Magdalane's Youth Club and Seaham G. F. S. Choral singing was contributed by the Junior Girls Training Corps. On the following night there were further plays produced by the St. Mary Magdalene's Boy's Club and again the Junior Girls Training Corps lent their voices to the evenings entertainment.

At the beginning of April Seaham Urban Council reduced the rate by 3d in the £ on the half year. Also at this time the Housing Committee declared that when labour was available the chimney sweeping service would be extended to include private property as well as council owned. Chimney sweeping had been in operation for some time as part of the Council's housing maintenance scheme. A number of people had been unfortunate to have been up before the magistrates for having chimney fires. A chimney fire during wartime could prove dangerous.

An agreement was reached between the Mine Worker's Federation and the National Coal Owners on the question of holiday pay. Adult workers over 21 would be receiving £5-5s-0d for the week's holiday and those between 18 and 21 would get £4-4s-0d and workers under 18 would be paid £3-3s-0d.

The Durham Miner's Rehabilitation Centre at 'The Hermitage' in Chester-le-Street opened on 10 April and took in its first patients. The centre was under the direction of the eminent surgeon Mr. C. Gordon Irwin.

This week Mrs. W. L. Kitchen of Longnewton Street, Dawdon, had word to say that her son, Flight Sergeant Bernard Kitchen had been commissioned in the Royal Air Force. A former pupil of St. Joseph's School and Ryhope Secondary School he had been in the R.A.F. since 1941 and gained his wings the following year. His father was serving in the Royal Artillery and his sister was a corporal in the W.A.A.F.

Colliery pollution of Murton Beck or Dawdon Dene Burn was again causing concern. One day the burn was flowing as black as ink and the next day it would be chalky white. The law on this kind of industrial pollution was seen as difficult to be acted upon but the money that the Council had spent on its park was being spoiled by this pollution.

Miss Isobel Baillie the well known soprano paid a return visit to Seaham on 11 April. Miss Baillie performed in the Church Street Methodist Church and was accompanied by the Seaham tenor, Mr. Jack Wick and the United Church Choir in the circuit.

The Seaham 'Penny a Week' Committee of the British Red Cross raised more than £100 per month and since 1943 had totalled £1,700. An exhibition was being held to draw attention to this fund. Premises for the exhibition were loaned by Mrs. Rubens in the Church Street Arcade and exhibits included a captured German flag, a captured Italian flag and a copy of General Montgomery's famous, 'Drive the enemy into the sea' message to the 8th Army. There was a charge of 3d to view the exhibition and all the proceeds went to The Duke of Gloucester's Fund.

There was a production of the Passion Play, 'The Upper Room' on Good Friday and Easter Sunday. The play, produced by St. Mary Magdalen's Youth Movement, was a great success. Experience gained by these young people on stage gave them much encouragement as a number of them entered the Seaham District Youth Organisation's public speaking competition. St. Mary Magdalen's members carried off seven awards.

By the middle of the month work on removing the road barriers was well under way throughout the area. One of the barriers which had not been scheduled for removal was the one at the top of Castlereagh Road and Londonderry Road. This barrier was not a vehicular road way and was only for pedestrians to pass through. The dog leg path through this huge concrete barrier was known as 'the hole in the wall.' Plans for a new roadway would by-pass the barrier so it was felt that the obstruction could be left as it was for the time being. In any case the new road scheme would not be completed until after the war.

'Salute the Soldier Week' Began on 29 April and a target had been set to raise £75,000. A number of events and entertainment's were taking place this week and Seaham and District Youth Organisations had taken on most of the organising of this event. There was a drama evening on Monday 1 May in the Rock House Hall. Among those taking part were Mrs F. L. Armstrong's Amateur Drama Company who were doing 'Property of the State.' Seaham and Dawdon Townswomen's Guild produced 'In Waltz Time', the Rock House Players did 'Genis Hominum' and excerpts from Romeo and Juliet and Seaham Central T G produced 'It's a Small World.' Mrs J Gentles produced the last three of these plays.

At the beginning of May a Seaham merchant seaman, Mr Arthur Mullaney of 13 Duke Street, Seaham was awarded the Silver Medal and Certificate of the Royal Society for the Prevention of Cruelty to Animals. While in a west coast port he had found a cat struggling in deep water in the dock and he dived in to rescue it. Other members of the crew who assisted Mr Mullaney received the Certificate. Mr Mullaney had been serving in the Merchant Navy for nine years and had been twice torpedoed.

At this time tests on air raid warning sirens had been conducted monthly and because this involved a good deal of time and manpower the Regional Commander decided the time was right for these tests to be reduced to one each quarter. The next test would be the first Monday in July.

Mr Shinwell attended a May Day Rally organised by the Seaham Labour Party in the Theatre Royal, Seaham on Sunday 7 May. Earlier Mr Shinwell opened a 'Salute the Soldier' variety entertainment at the Empire Theatre. The emphasis was on the 'Free Gift Fund' and the show was produced by Mrs F. L. Armstrong. Mr Shinwell said, "Whatever could be done to encourage the men in the forces should be done, particularly on the eve of the greatest trials this country has ever faced." The total amount raised over the week came to £82,000 and this exceeded the target by £7,000.

Seaham Housing Committee were setting up a team of house-to-house canvassers, on the suggestion of the Ministry of Health, to look into the lodging of trainee miners. The wages of these canvassers was paid by the Ministry of Health.

The Church Lads Brigade at Dawdon received their new instruments at the beginning of the month and were putting in extra practice at the Green Drive and at Dawdon Dene.

The band tutor was Mr Norman Henderson.

News from Changi Prisoner of War Camp was received by the Reverend James Duncan in a letter from a relative of one of the officers imprisoned at the camp. Post cards had been received from prisoners acknowledging receipt of letters from home. Drugs and medicine had been taken by a returning exchange ship and they had been landed at Singapore before Christmas.

A year on from a very damaging air attack on Seaham had seen some changes. One of the buildings that had been damaged was the Presbyterian Church and because the building was unsafe it had to be demolished. The school room, however, had been left intact and services had been conducted in there.

New ration books were being issued on Monday 22 May and about 24,000 books were processed by a staff of six with the help of two members of the Citizens Advice Bureau.

The Whit Monday turned out to be one of the finest for many years. Dawdon Dene was packed with people enjoying walking through to Dalton-le-Dale along the lane which was ablaze with Laburnum and Hawthorn blossom. However, the burn running through this area was now disappearing down a large hole and the rest of the stream bed was almost dry. This phenomenon had happened many years ago and the stream bed had had to be reinforced with concrete.

Seaham Housing Committee had been invited to inspect a new factory built house in London but as this would have meant much travelling it was felt that a similar house should be erected in the North East.

Over the past months there had been many military activities going on. Manoeuvres around Seaham were going ahead with Brengun Carriers racing along Stockton Road and troops carrying out mock attacks. Many corners of streets had a soldier lying on the ground with his 303 rifle to his shoulder while inquisitive children stood around him watching. In one exercise a group of children playing in the 'Hollow', a pathway leading from Mount Pleasant to Dalton-le-Dale, spotted a group of soldiers with yellow armbands near the south end of the village. The children reported this to soldiers with a different coloured armband gathered on Stockton Road near West Farm. The information was gratefully received as these soldiers moved off to the 'attack.' Perhaps the use of information given by children would prove invaluable when these same troops were at last fighting in France.

H.M.S. Seaham had returned to England from the Mediterranean docking at Falmouth on 2 January. Over the next three months she had repairs undertaken by Lilley-Cox of Falmouth. During this time the ship's company had a collection to raise money to buy a silver cup for the children of Seaham High Colliery School. The cup was bought at a London jewellers and sent to the school with a letter of gratitude to the children for their kindness in sending parcels to the men and for writing letters of encouragement while 'their' ship was on active service.

Chapter 6, 1944

In the late hours of 5 June, H.M.S. Seaham with other minesweepers quietly slipped out into the English Channel and headed for the French coast. These ships were to sweep the mines from the lanes which would soon be filled with the D-Day armada as dawn broke that historic day, 6 June. Following on from this, important constructions of the Mulberry Harbour which had been made at the Compton and Harrison works in the town, were floated into place along with other components made in other places such as Middlesbrough and all taken to the South Coast ready for the big day, D-Day.

At an investiture this week, A.B. Ernest Brady Turner (21) serving in the Royal Navy, received the Distinguished Service Medal from the King. The award was made for gallantry and devotion to duty while serving on a motor launch. A.B. Turner had been badly wounded in an enemy air attack off Crete. Before joining the navy he had worked at Seaham Docks.

Local Councillor, Mrs M.I. Robinson, received the sad news in the middle of June that her youngest son, Corporal Robert Donkin Robinson, had been killed in action in Burma. Corporal Robinson had been an apprentice with Seaham Urban Council until he was called up.

A Seaham airman, Sergeant Raynolds, of a Serving Commando Unit of the R.A.F., was in the news after capturing a German soldier after the invasion of France. He had been on leave in Seaham shortly before D-Day and his parents were unaware that he was now in France.

By the end of June the new 'Prefabricated House' was in full production. These exciting homes with their modern kitchens were an interesting novelty in the town and were design to last for about ten years.

New Seaham Rabbit and Cavy Club held its monthly show in the first week of July with an entry of over one hundred rabbits which were described as the cream of the North East. Much of the success of the club was said to be due to the hard work done by the secretary, Tom Robson.

'The Children's Theatre' paid a visit to the Theatre Royal on Saturday 8 July. School children from local schools filled the theatre and enjoyed dramatised nursery rhymes performed by the enthusiastic cast.

Private H. Foggon (24) son of a local newsagent was recovering in hospital in Scotland after being blown up by a shell in Normandy. After joining the army four years earlier he was one of those who had been evacuated from Dunkirk. After some time back in England he was sent to North Africa and went through to Tunis. After special training he was again in action in the second wave in the landings on D-Day and had been in France for a month until his luck ran out.

Seaham man, Sergeant Ernest Richardson R.A., serving in Scotland was awarded the B.E.M. in the second week of July and Pilot Officer Thomas Barrow, of Beech Crescent, Seaham won his commission in the R.A.F. P/O. Barrow had been in County Durham Police Force before joining the R.A.F.

'And Miles to go Before I Sleep'

On Saturday 29 July part of the beach at Seaham was reopened to the public to the great delight of the children of the town. There was a new access road, built by the Town Council, from the cliff top to the sands below. After having been closed for five years and cordoned off with barbed wire and 'mine warning' boards many children had never set foot in the sea before. There were still some restrictions but as long as the public obeyed the rules that part of the beach would remain open. Opening hours were from 9 a.m. to 9 p.m. throughout the summer. The British Restaurant provided teas and sandwiches from a hut on the cliff top.

A letter from H.M.S. Seaham to the Head Mistress of Seaham High Colliery School, Miss Blanch Foxhall, thanked all the pupils and staff of the school for all the parcels sent to the crew over the years. 'Please pass on the sincere thanks of the entire ship's company to your pupils for the parcels that they so generously sent.' A silver cup sent by the ship's company from a London jewellers arrived at the school and the first sports day saw the cup presented to the winning team by Coun. Mrs. T. Todd.

A number of pubs in the town over the holiday period were showing 'no beer' signs after their pumps ran dry because of great demand.

Durham County Council was threatening to close the grounds of Seaham Hall because of damage being done in the area by a section of the public. Wanton destruction of fences around the Hall was unacceptable and there were reports that some youths had been seen throwing rocks from the bridge on to the footpath below. This was a very dangerous practice and together with the rowdyism that was being blamed on these youths, some action would have to be taken. The disturbance to staff and patients in the hospital was becoming intolerable. Lord Londonderry had handed over Seaham Hall on the understanding that the public would be allowed the use of the grounds but he now agreed that disciplinary action should be taken in the interests of the health of the patients.

Mr. Lawrence Scollen of The Avenue, Seaham had recently recorded a talk in French for the B.B.C. This was broadcast on the French labour talks programme. During the talk, Mr Scollen spoke of the efforts that were being made by the miners of Durham to produce more coal for the production of munitions, the post-war outlook and how there would be a need for great co-operation between nations when the present conflict came to an end.

School holidays were nearly over and the children had for the first time in years been able to enjoy themselves on the beach at Seaham. During the fine weather hundreds of families had picnicked on the sands, hot water was available to make a cup of tea and an old ambulance manned by Red Cross volunteers and junior members stood in readiness on the cliff top to treat jelly fish stings or minor cuts if necessary.

On 19 August an exhibition of photographs went on show in Sunderland showing the local history of the area. A number of photographs from Seaham residents was also included and these had been compiled by Mr. John McCutchion, the Librarian. The public had been asked to help by lending any photographs they might have with the only provision that they were taken before 1914. Thirty three photographs of Seaham were exhibited.

Chapter 6, 1944

The 26th Seaham Battalion of the Home Guard held a 'Military Sports' event at the Cricket Ground in Seaham Harbour on Saturday 24 August in aid of The British Red Cross. There were a number of different sporting activities and a good attendance brought much needed funds for a good cause.

Also this week a 'Children's Sports' event was held on Deneside Football Ground. This was the first time this event had taken place and the idea had been suggested by Coun. Winter. The committee organising the sports had set about raising money for the event and had soon collected £40.

The two day programme was attended by about 500 people each day; attractive prises were presented to winners. At the end of the games there was a balance of £8 which was carried forward to start a fund for the 'Victory Sports' when the town would celebrate peace again.

Sad news arrived in Seaham at the end of August of the death of Sergeant Bert Hillam R.A., of Jasper Avenue, Seaham. After being involved in the fighting at El Alamein and Sicily he had been wounded in the initial landings in Italy but had returned to duty after seven weeks. In August he was severely wounded and died in hospital four days later.

During the first week in September it was learned that the Assistant Cub Master of the 5th Seaham (Christ Church) Scout Group, had died in Italy. Mr Edward Marwood Rooney of Gregson Terrace, Seaham had been a member of the Seaham Group for more than ten years. Mr Rooney had served in the Middle East for four and a half years with the Royal Corps of Signals.

The Colonial Secretary has informed the Reverend James Duncan that a message was picked up from a Japanese control station in Singapore from Mrs Graham White and contained the words 'both well'. The news that the Venerable Graham White and his wife were in reasonably good health was a great tonic for the local church community.

The middle of September brought the good news that the 'Black Out' was ended by the switching on of nearly 300 street lamps. These lights were known as 'moon lighting' and at the appointed time children gathered around these lamps ready for the great switch on. Black out in the homes was relaxed but there was some confusion brought about by a local newspaper which had stated that the relaxation of the black out did not include Seaham.

On the weekend of 24 and 25 September, Mr Emanuel Shinwell M.P. was very busy with speaking engagements. After speaking to the Engineering Industries Association in London on Thursday he travelled overnight to attend a meeting of Durham County Urban Council Association at Durham on Friday after noon. He then addressed a meeting of the Executive Committee of the Seaham Labour Party on Friday night. in Easington. Saturday morning saw him receiving a deputation at Seaham from the National Association of Headmasters then in the afternoon he was addressing a delegate conference of Seaham Divisional Labour Party. He then returned to London to a speaking engagement to the London Co-operative Society on Sunday.

Sergeant Richard John Mitchell R.A.F. arrived home at the beginning of October after being missing for about five months. Sergeant Mitchell, whose home is at 12 Grant Crescent, Seaham, was formerly a miner at Dawdon Colliery but was now a mid-upper gunner with a Lancaster bomber crew in the R.A.F. In a raid over Germany last April his aircraft was hit and set on fire. He was ordered to bail out and landed in a wood somewhere near the French/German border. On landing he hurt his back and leg and just wondered about the wood for three days. He finally got across in to France before passing out with exhaustion. When he came to he was being cared for by a group of French people. He was handed on to a Doctor who looked after him in his home for three weeks. After hearing of the relief of Paris Sergeant Mitchell decided to try his luck to get home. He journeyed to Marseilles, Italy, North Africa, Cornwall and London and finally made it back to Seaham.

The Lord street subway, which had been damaged by a bomb in 1943 was now the centre of concern this week when it was found that boys were climbing through the barbed wire fence on to the mineral railway line. The subway had been repaired so that trucks could again get to the docks but the barbed wire fence was proving to be inadequate and local residents said that it was to easy for children to get on to the line.

Another military honour was won by Squadron Leader William Geffrey Rees R.A.F.V.R. who was born in Seaham. This time he had been awarded a Bar to his D.F.C. which he won in 1941.

A very sad incident occurred on the evening of 17 October in the skies over Seaham and Murton. A Whitley V bomber, Serial AD685, from No. 19 Operational Training Unit at R.A.F. Kinloss was taking part in a night cross country exercise. It passed over Seaham at a height of 4,000 to 5,000 feet flying through cumulus nimbus cloud. It would seem that turbulence and icing of the wings caused a failure of the airframe and the aircraft broke up. AD685 was recorded as missing at 21.45 hours.

Police arrived at Mr Bill Bulmer's Stotfold Farm to inform him that an aircraft was missing and would he help with others to search his land and neighbouring Slingley Hill Farm land for possible survivors. Unfortunately there were no survivors. The crew were all found in and around the fuselage which was in an upside down position near to Slingley Hill Farm. The two engines had fallen into a field just south of Roy Snowdon's field locally known as the Bull Field. One wing came to rest against a back yard wall in Mount Pleasant, Seaham and the other wing against the George Inn on The Avenue. The R.A.F. took the wreckage away on a long trailer two days later.

The Pilot was Flying Officer Kenneth Reed of the Royal Canadian Air Force, son of Thomas Matthew and Ethel Reed of Edmunton, Alberta.

The navigator was Flying Officer Walter Douglas Wall (20) R.C.A.F. and the son of Walter A. Wall and Isobelle Wall of Ontario.

Mid-Upper Gunner was Pilot Officer Alexander Lorne Sunstrum (22) R.C.A.F. and the son of Alexander and Jeanne Cove Sunstrum of Cochrane, Ontario.

Chapter 6, 1944

Air Bomber was Sergeant Leslie John Olmstead (29) R.C.A.F. and the son of Leslie John and Katherine Sarah Olmstead and the husband of Laura Katherine Olmstead of Estlin, Saskatchewan.

Air Gunner was John Frederich Dowding (17) R.C.A.F. and the son of Ivan L and Rhea J Dowding of Sarnia, Ontario.

Wireless Operator was Sergeant Ernest William Leivers (19) R.A.F. the only British member of the crew and son of Cyril Pannett Leivers and Ethel Mary Leivers of Derbyshire.

The Canadian members of the crew were all buried with full military honours at Stonegate Cemetery, Harrogate (Section G, Row A, No.5.6.7.8. and 9.)

Sergeant Leivers was interred in Normanton Cemetery. (Grave 2754)

An inscription at the foot of seventeen year old P.O. Dowdings headstone reads, "He challenged those who would destroy the innocent and the way of life that he loved so well."

The Commanding Officer of Seaham Air Training Corps, Conc. J.C. Jennings left Seaham at the beginning of November to take up a post of Headmaster of Netherseal Church of England School, Burton-on-Trent. Mr Jennings had been a member of the Town Council for seven years. It was his initiative three years earlier that saw the setting up of the Seaham Squadron of the Air Training Corps and he became the Commanding Officer with the rank of Flight Lieutenant.

In the Rock House Community Centre on Wednesday 8 a meeting was held to form a committee to look into the welfare of old people. Other towns had set up such organisations and it was felt that Seaham should also be part of this trend. Rock House had provided entertainment for old people for a number of years during the winter months. This kind of work with pensioners would now be extended to all old or infirm people in the town.

People were making plans for the town after the war was over and there was a suggestion put to the Seaham Highways Committee by the surveyor that an open shopping area might be created by the removal of parts of Vane Terrace, Henry Street, and Adelaide Row. North and South Railway Street had once been two of the towns main shopping streets but this was no longer the case.

In the middle of November word was received that Lance Corporal E.J. Watson (24), who had been a prisoner of war in Germany since 1940, was now missing and presumed dead after aerial bombardment. Lance Corporal Watson was a regular soldier who had joined up in 1938 after working at Vane Tempest Colliery. He had been captured in France in the rearguard while covering the retreat towards Dunkirk in May 1940.

By the end of the month there was an exhibition by the Rock House Art Club of paintings and drawings held in the centre. Paintings in oil and water colour as well as black and white sketches were of a very high standard and the artists won praise from those who visited the exhibition.

'And Miles to go Before I Sleep'

The General Committee of the 'Welcome Home Fund' set themselves a target of £5,000 to be raised before the end of the war and £1,000 by the end of December. The recent Chrysanthemum Show held in Dawdon Miner's Hall raised money on behalf of the fund and a variety show composed of local artists was held at the Empire Theatre, Seaham on Saturday afternoon 26 November. This raised £65.

At an investiture at Buckingham Palace this week, Mr Robert Copeland, Marine Engineer of Queen Street, Seaham was awarded the O.B.E. for Meritorious Service at sea. Mr Copeland had been serving with the Tanfeild Shipping Company of Newcastle for the whole of the war.

The Home Guard was 'stood down' on Sunday 3 December after serving their communities since May 1940. The 26th Seaham Battalion of the Homeguard was first called the Local Defence Volunteers and on being formed drilled in the British Legion Club in Londonderry Road then they used the lawns in Rock House dene for drill and as a rifle range. In the beginning there were no uniforms only the L.D.V. armbands which each member wore. The local collieries lent the battalion wooden pick shafts that would have to do until real rifles were made available.

Dawdon Colliery buzzer sounded for the first time since the beginning of the war. It had been used as an air raid warning in the very early days of the war but on the 4 December it was again in service for industrial purposes.

An air compressor was bought by the Urban Council ready to start on the work of removing the road barriers in the town. Estimates of the cost of doing this work had been forwarded to the Ministry of Road Transport and the Council were just awaiting their permission to go ahead.

On Wednesday 13 December there was a Christmas Gift payout for the Seaham Colliery Aged Miners at the Miner's Hall, New Seaham and also at the Miner's Hall, Dawdon for Dawdon Aged Miners on the same afternoon.

On the evening of Thursday 21 December the National Association of Local Government Officers organised an exhibition of table tennis played by several International class players. This exhibition was held in the Dawdon Miner's Hall and all money raised was given to the 'Welcome Home' fund.

Towards the end of December, the W.V.S. in Seaham received another 10lbs of wool to be knitted into pullovers for prisoners of war. There was also material sufficient to make 50 sleeping gowns for children of occupied countries. Also, the W.V.S. were asking for donations of furniture, bedding and other household goods under the 'Good Neighbour' scheme. These items were to be sent to the Borough of Poplar in London which had been adopted by the Northern Region.

Another initiative in the 'Welcome Home' fund raising effort was that of the National and Local Government Officers. They organised a dance held in the Drill Hall on 28

Chapter 6, 1944

December by kind permission of Col. R.L.S. Pemberton and the music was provided by The Royal Armoured Corps Dance Orchestra.

The Reverend O.N. Gwilliam sent the following Christmas message to the 'Lads and Girls in the forces.'

"We are sending you this from the Church in Seaham with our very best wishes for you wherever you are this Christmas and wish sincere greetings from all the folk here in Seaham. May this Christmas be full of good cheer for you and yours and may 1945 see the finish of this war with a great victory to round off all the years of struggle and sacrifice. And then may we see the safe and welcome return home of all those who have been so far away and so long absent from the old home and friends."

This Christmas greeting was sent to men and women in India, Africa, Italy, Egypt, Burma and to those at sea.

Dawdon Youth Fellowship spent Christmas Eve singing Christmas Carols on visits to a number of places in the district. There was a feeling that, perhaps, next Christmas would see peace and good will to all men.

A local craftsman made a gift of eight beautiful collecting plates for St. John's Church, Seaham. These plates were dedicated by the vicar, the Reverend O.N. Gwilliam and were used at the service for the first time on Christmas Day.

A Christmas letter was received by Mr. J.C. Edington, Secretary of the Seaham Savings Committee from the Commander of H.M.S. Seaham the warship that had been adopted by the town following 'Warship Week.' The letter reads:-

"May I take this opportunity on behalf of the officers and men of H.M.S. Seaham to wish all our friends in Seaham a Happy Christmas.

Over the past year we have appreciated very much the very thoughtful and generous gifts which it has been our pleasure to receive and we have been particularly moved by the gifts from the children of New Seaham High Colliery School. It speaks very well for the people responsible for their training and upbringing that these children, who cannot have much to give, should give so generously.

We look forward with hope that the New Year will bring peace in a world that sorely needs it. Again, thanking you and wishing the best of luck to all at Seaham from H.M.S. Seaham."

From a recent savings week a quantity of cigarettes was sent to the crew.

Chapter 7, 1945

The End of the Nightmare

There was concern expressed by Police Superintendent Proud at Seaham Brewster's Sessions when he drew attention to the licensees selling intoxicating alcohol for consumption on the premises in the 'off sales' department of public houses. The objection was that they were not properly supervised. The places where these practices were being carried out were commonly known as the 'bottle and jug' department and one 15 year old had been found drinking alcohol in one of these places. Superintendent Proud said that these places were generally small and dimly lit and that liquor is served through an aperture.

Saturday 10 February saw the Sadlers Wells Opera Company visiting Seaham in the form of Victoria Sladen (Soprano) and Edith Coates (Contralto) at a celebrity concert in the Church Street Methodist Church, Seaham. An augmented choir took part in the concert conducted by Mr J.W. Kelly with Mrs Kelly at the organ.

Another CEMA concert was held this weekend in the Parish Hall, Seaham on Sunday evening. Artists included Miss Margaret Field Hyde (Soprano), Mr John Francis (Flute), Mr George Roth (Cello) and Miss Marie Korchinaka (Harp).

Lord Londonderry visited his Dawdon Colliery on Friday 9 February and congratulated the manager and staff of the Production Committee for beating their coal production target for the second week running.

On the following evening the Marquis attended a performance of 'Ali Baba and the Forty Thieves' at the Theatre Royal. The show was produced by the Seaham Amateur Operatic Society and a bouquet was presented by the Marquis to Miss Betty Davidson who took the part of Mrs Ali Baba. The bouquet was made up of orchids from the Wynyard Estate of the Marquis at Wolviston.

On Sunday afternoon, the Marquis visited Seaham Hall Sanatorium and, on a tour of the hospital, spoke to the 130 patients.

Mr Emanuel Shinwell M.P. wrote to a friend in Seaham this week telling him that he was just getting over the worst bout of 'flue that he had ever had. He said that he was now behind in his letter writing as he usually got between 300 and 400 letters each week. Many of the letters were from people in the forces and a good many from Seaham folk.

Mr J. Worthington, Surveyor to Seaham Urban Council, was stressing that there was still a great need for salvage. Paper, bones and kitchen waste were still needed and he said that the Council had 64 pigs being reared on kitchen waste.

Mr E Shinwell asked the President of the Board of Trade if he had yet considered the proposal sent to him by Seaham Urban Council that there should be more thought to the provision of industries in the town. Mr Hugh Dalton answering the question in the House said that he had not yet received the communication but that he would be glad to consider any representation the Council might make.

A Seaham man now resident in Buffalo, U.S.A. and serving in the U.S. Army in Belgium, Sergeant Robert Watson Potts, was awarded military honours in the form of the American Bronze Star. This was awarded for heroic service against the enemy while under heavy artillery fire when he left his foxhole to rescue nine men who had been wounded by mortar fire. The award was endorsed by the President of the United States and was presented this month to Sergeant Potts by General Patton at a parade at the Front.

Corporal Jack Bell (26) of Coronation Buildings, Seaham who had been in a prisoner of war camp in Germany was reported to have died there in February. He had been captured and had then escaped but later was captured and sent to Germany.

Mr Frank E. Franks the well know comedian and promoter visited Murton in order to see the production of 'The Belle of New York' put on by the Murton Amateur Operatic Society. He said that the show was the best that he had ever seen and that many of the professional companies could not have surpassed their performance. Mr Franks had started his stage career in the same theatre, The Empire Theatre, 32 years earlier.

Because of the new 'modified' street lighting figures released at the beginning of March showed a big reduction in road traffic accidents for January and February. There were 11 fatal accidents in County Durham in those two months compared with 24 for the same two months of the previous year.

Word was received at the beginning of March by Mr and Mrs William Aitkin of Grant Crescent, Seaham that their son, Private Geoffrey Aitkin who was a prisoner of war in Stalag XXA in Poland had been freed and was now in Allied hands; he had been released from captivity by the advancing Russian Army. It was believed, from reports at the time, that he was already at sea and on his way home. Private Aitkin had been in the North Staffs Regimental Band and while in captivity had spent some of his time composing a number of pieces of band music. He had been able to send some of these home and some had already been used in concerts by the Regimental Band.

A Naval Gunner from Antrim, Northern Ireland, was drowned in Seaham Dock this month. He had been on an all day drinking session with his shipmate after being paid and in the darkened conditions of the dock had fallen of the quay and into the water. His body was recovered some time later.

A message from the Belgian Red Cross asked the Seaham W.V.S. if they would be kind enough to distribute some toys sent by Belgian children to British children who had lost their fathers in the war. This included the forces, Civil Defence Forces and those whose fathers were prisoners of war.

Two Seaham brothers, Driver Louis Questa R.A.S.C. and his brother George met in Florence while they were standing in a queue waiting for a cup of tea. George was spending a leave in Florence and Louis was already stationed there; they had not met for four years. George had been at Dunkirk then Malta and Italy while Louis had served in North Africa and Italy.

At the end of the month Seaham Council put out a notice that those people who intended to visit the beach should not pick up any strange objects that might be washed up by the tide nor should they go where there were notices prohibiting entry. Visitors to the beach from the Featherbed Rock northward did so at their own risk.

Great news was received by Mr and Mrs E.J. Watson of 65 Bethune Avenue, Seaham this week. their son, Lance-Corporal E.J.Watson who had been a prisoner of war and was thought to have been killed as the result of an aerial bombardment was reported, through his Regimental Record Office, to be alive and now in Allied hands. He was to be sent home as soon as possible.

Three young men were fined for being on the beach south of the Featherbed Rock. The restrictions were still in force for that area and access between Featherbed Rock and Noses Point was out of bounds to all. The beach area north of Featherbed Rock was quite adequate for those who wished to enjoy sea and sand.

Seaham Urban Council received an offer from the Government at the beginning of April of fifty prefabricated houses of the American design and this offer was accepted. There would be a great need for housing when service men and women began to return after the war and this was seen as a good start.

The chance of football returning to normal in the coming season was being seriously considered by the big clubs. Two Murton Colliery Welfare players were snapped up by Huddersfield Town at this time. Bob Owen (20), left half, had signed as had Billy Drake, inside left, two gifted players who would be missed by the Murton team.

Mr Douglas Murry of The Dene, Seaham the well known horse breeder, had another great win at the County Agricultural Society Show in April with his Clydesdale filly, 'Seaham Lady Athenia' as supreme champion. After this success the filly was sold to Mr Joseph Armstrong for his stud in Cumberland.

Also in April, Captain John Burnham (53) R.A. of Smallbrook, North Dene Avenue, Seaham was awarded the M.B.E. (Military Division) for gallantry and distinguished service in Italy.

Before the war Captain Burnham had been involved with Seaham Amateur Operatic

Society as secretary and also taking lead rolls in a number of productions.

The Methodist Church was sensing victory by now and by the end of April had declared that on the day that hostilities ceased their churches would throw their doors open for private prayer and on the second day a thanksgiving service would be held in the Church Street Methodists Church at 11 a.m.

A procession was to leave Parkside at 10.15 a.m. for the Church Street service and another procession would leave Mount Pleasant at the same time for a thanksgiving service at the Jubilee Methodist Church, New Seaham.

Sergeant Thomas William Summerbell R.A.F., son of Mr and Mrs Thomas Summerbell of 5 Strangways Street, Dawdon won his wings as Flight Engineer. He joined the R.A.F. in 1943 after being employed as a bricklayer at Dawdon Colliery. His flying interest was nurtured in the Air Training Corps where he had gained the rank of Flight Sergeant. He was soon to be married to Private B. Wallace A.T.S. of 35 Strangways Street.

In the last week of April, the landlord of the Golden Lion pub in Seaham, Mr Jack Stuart, handed over a cheque for 100 guineas at a meeting in the pub that had been raised by patrons of the Golden Lion, to Counc. S. Barrett, Chairman of the 'Welcome Home' fund. Mr Sid Gilmore handed over a further £35 on behalf of the Seaham Dance Club. With a target of £5,000 the fund already stood at £2,000 raised since September.

The good work of Seaham Amateur Operatic Society continued with donations being given to a number of charities from money raised in their successful production of Ali Baba.

The Prime Minister, Mr Winston Churchill, broadcast to the Nation on B.B.C radio at 3p.m. on Tuesday 8 May that the German High Command had signed an Act of Unconditional Surrender of all land, sea and air forces in Europe to the Allied Expeditionary Force at 2.41 a.m. Mr Churchill continued :-

"Gratitude to all our splendid Allies goes forth from all our hearts in these islands and throughout the British Empire. We may allow ourselves a brief period of rejoicing but let us not forget for a moment the toils and effort that lie ahead."

Japan was still waging war and there were months of struggle ahead. Mr Churchill went on :-

"We must now devote all our strength and all our resources to the completion of our task both at home and abroad. Advance Britannia, Long live the cause of freedom, God Save the King."

The following day flags were flying on all of the streets and celebrations began. The atmosphere was electric and everyone seemed to have a smile on their face. The war in Europe was over.

In Murton, after the Prime Minister's speech, a procession lead by Murton Prize Band paraded through the streets carrying an effigy of Adolf Hitler with an inscription which read, 'WE HAVE THE PLEASURE TO ANNOUNCE THAT WE WILL EXECUTE THIS BASTARD AT MIDNIGHT TO NIGHT.'

This proclamation was carried out at the appointed hour.

Every piece of open land had bonfires built and in some cases people brought out pianos into the streets and a general 'knees up' carried on until breakfast time.

The film programme at Murton's Rex Theatre on Wednesday was cancelled and the doors were thrown open for a concert and a singing contest with the audience deciding the winners. Mr G.M. Hall set up broadcasting equipment so that those who could not get into the theatre could listen to the concert outside. The King's speech was also broadcast to those outside the theatre.

The Licensed Victuallers Association had not applied for an extension of licensing hours because of a shortage of supplies. There had been a number of statements about opening hours and this had lead to confusion with some of the public.

Many streets were decorated and street parties were the order of the day. Between Jubilee Avenue and Queens Avenue, Seaham tables were set up and a wonderful tea was provided. After everyone had had their fill tables were moved away and the children had games and races organised by the adults. Suddenly someone spotted a man going past the end of the street to a house in Queens Avenue. He had been a prisoner of war in one of the Stalag camps. Everyone gathered around him cheering and patting him on the back. However, one lady had the sad task of telling him that his mother was very ill.

Whit Monday saw many people heading to the Stockton Races by train. The trains from Seaham heading south were packed with people and even the corridors were full. The midday express from Sunderland could not take any more passengers but the railway managed to put on a relief train ten minutes later.

Captain Maurice Victor MacMillan was selected by Seaham Conservative Association as the prospective candidate for Seaham in the forthcoming General Election. Captain MacMillan was the only son of Mr Harold MacMillan, Conservative member for Stockton and Secretary of State for Air in Mr Churchill's Government.

Mr Richard Bainbridge, Headmaster of Seaham Church of England School retired at the end of May. Mr Bainbridge, who was also the choir master at St. John's Church, had already extended his working life because of the shortage of teachers through many of them being away in the services.

The Seaham Girls Training Corps., with Horden, Easington, Houghton and Hetton groups adopted the small village of Renkum in the Netherlands in the Arnhem district. When the Germans withdrew the village was badly damaged and much of what the villages had had been taken. The inhabitants were in a very sorry state though food was being provided from elsewhere there was still a great need for clothing and underwear for children, wool and kitchenware.

On 12 June the G.T.C. held a bring and buy sale in the Seaham Girls Grammar School to raise funds for this village and to collect gifts of clothing not intended for sale.

The third official holiday to celebrate victory was declared for Monday 18 June. All schools and collieries were closed and there were tea parties for children and entertainment for pensioner were part of the days festivities.

Two brothers from Seaham arrived home in the middle of the month after being released from captivity. They were Privates John and Albert Hay D.L.I. of 19 Caroline Street. John had been captured at Cos in the Dodecanese Islands and had been held prisoner for 14 months. Albert was first in Italian hands for 2 years and then held by the Germans for 2 years.

An application by the owner of a number of donkeys for permission to use the beach to give rides to children was received by Seaham Urban Council at the end of the month. The Council were quite happy with the idea but pointed out to the applicant that the Agent for the Marquis of Londonderry would also have to give his permission.

Footpath barriers in Dawdon Dene, a wartime defensive measure were removed and people walking through to Dalton-le-Dale could now use the path without hindrance.

At the beginning of July a Sergeant Swaby of Anfield Plain wrote to members of Seaham G.T.C. confirming the terrible state of the villagers of Renkum in Holland. Sergeant Swaby was stationed near the village and he had news from home about the efforts of the G.T.C. to help the village. He said that, apart from the damage to their homes, the German troops had taken not only valuables but also bedding and even floorboards from houses to use in defensive trenches.

The Ministry of Education took over part of Lord Londonderry's Wynyard Hall as a teacher training college. The Marquis continued to reside in part of the Hall and would do so when the first students arrive in September. Over the last few years of the war the military authorities and the National Fire Service had occupied Wynyard Hall.

On the 26 July Mr Emanuel Shinwell was re-elected as Member of Parliament for Seaham when a landslide victory for the Labour Party saw 393 Labour members returned. Mr Shinwell received 42,942 votes, Mr Maurice MacMillan (Con) 10,685 votes and Mr Shinwell was returned with a majority of 32,257. After the jubilation in the Seaham constituency Mr Shinwell returned to London and was promptly sent for by Mr Attlee the new Prime Minister. Mr Attlee said to Shinwell, "I want you to take the Ministry of Fuel and Power and the job will include nationalizing the mines. You will be in the Cabinet."

The first week of August had 200 cadets and 30 officers of the Seaham Cadet Battalion, 12th Durham Light Infantry attending camp at the 61st Training Regiment, R.A.C. at

Streatham, Barnard Castle. The Battalion was a combined unit drawn from Seaham, Dawdon, Murton, Ryhope, Silksworth and South Hylton and was under the command of Major J. Elliott of Seaham.

During this week long camp a Seaham cadet had the remarkable experience of trying to save the life of another cadet. Cadet K. W. Thornton of Blackhall Colliery had gone for a swim in the river Tees but got into difficulties. It was some time before Cadet Thornton was located and taken out of the water. At this point Corporal R.E. Hodgson of Station Road, Seaham began artificial respiration and carried on for one and a half hours assisted by another officer. When a doctor arrived he declared that Cadet Thornton was dead. Corporal Hodgson was left in a very distressed state and received medical attention when he arrived back at camp but was hailed as a hero for his sustained efforts to save his comrade.

August the 6 Bank Holiday was a washout for the Second Annual Sports Day which was to have been held by the Seaham Colliery Recreation and Welfare Association in the Recreation Grounds, Seaham. The torrential downpour left the beaches deserted where there had been large crowds on the Saturday and Sunday. By Monday heavy seas forced the closure of the dock gates to shipping. This was a very rare occasion in the summer months though in winter an all to common thing.

On this day the first atomic bomb was dropped on Hiroshima, Japan and on the following Thursday the second atomic bomb was dropped on Nagasaki with horrendous results. This brought a surrender proclamation from the Imperial Palace on the 10 August.

Young 12 year old Les Alexander, of 17 Queens Avenue, Seaham was enjoying his first holiday in London on this day and as he walked through Leicester Square in the morning sunshine there was a sudden excitement as showers of ticker-tape began falling from high up office buildings. The word was out, the Japanese had surrendered. By the time young Les reached Piccadilly a man was standing on a street corner selling red, white and blue ribbons in a bow for 3d each. Crowds made there way to Downing Street to see the Prime Minister arrive from the House of Commons together with his Ministers for an urgent Cabinet meeting.

In the evening London was packed with hundreds of thousands of people celebrating the end of hostilities; civilians, soldiers sailors and airmen of all nationalities were on the streets dancing and singing largely lead by American servicemen.

On Tuesday night 14 August world peace returned. In a midnight speech announcing the surrender terms the Prime Minister, Mr Clement Attlee said :-

"The last of our enemies is laid low. Peace has once again come to the world. Let us thank God for this great deliverance and his mercy. Long Live the King."

The celebrations in Seaham and Murton mirrored those of earlier at the Victory in Europe celebrations. Bonfires and dancing in the streets continued until the early hours. Many shops were besieged for food and pubs ran dry as parties got underway.

Chapter 7, 1945

The long six years of struggle, hardship and danger were at last over. Many families in Seaham and Murton had lost loved ones but there was some consolation that their loss had not been in vain.

Chapter 8

H. M. S. SEAHAM

An announcement was made in December, 1941 that Seaham was to have a 'Warship Week' to raise funds to 'buy' a ship for the Royal Navy. 'Warship Week' was to take place between 7 and 14 February, 1942. This announcement was met with great excitement by the people of the town and if it was successful there would be something tangible that the towns folk could identify with, something that would be part of their answer to Nazism and the hope of an early end to the war. There was a long way to go before that dream would be realised.

The Seaham War Savings Committee Executive met to appoint a number of sub-committees to oversee various phases of the 'Warship Week' effort. The President of Seaham War Savings Committee, Coun. H.F. Lee, together with the Clerk to Seaham Urban District Council, Mr J.C.Edington, set out the possibilities for the local community in this savings drive.

The town was to be divided into group savings areas, shopping and business centres, industrial undertakings, schools, workshops and street groups. There were in existence at that time 120 savings associations within the urban area and the weekly total savings for Seaham was published in the Press. Though savings towards the war effort were good, the 'Warship Week' was focused as a special effort to intensify the fund raising. To help to bring about the involvement of all of the townspeople there would be special entertainment's and other functions arranged.

The Committee were told that the Admiralty had named a Minesweeper, H.M.S. Seaham and the vessel had already been launched at the shipbuilding yards of Lobnitz and Company of Renfrew in Scotland. A target worthy of the town was being asked for and it was felt that £65,000 could be raised and that the ship would be adopted by the town. With only about six weeks to go before 'Warship Week' the town would have to be ready to enter into the greatest financial campaign ever undertaken in Seaham.

At the end of April, 1942, the total amount of money raised in Seaham during 'Warship Week' was published and the magnificent figure of £101,691 was revealed. The War Savings Committee and the people of the town were rightfully proud of their achievement; H.M.S. Seaham was now their ship and she would play her part in the fight against Nazi Germany. The regional figure published for 'Warship Week' showed a total of £18,500,000. The people of Seaham and of the region had made a supreme effort.

Chapter 8,

Many local groups now wanted to continue their relationship with the Minesweeper and her crew. One such group was made up of the children of Seaham High Colliery School who included Tony Weirs, Alfie Partridge, Colin Stokoe, Norman and Ronnie Ferguson, Frank Miller, Robert Malcolm, Johnnie Doughty, Arnot Weightman, Bob Beattie, Jackie Greenwood, Anthony Simpson and also many of the girls who would be leaving the school to attend the Low Colliery Junior Girls School. All of the children of this school took to the task with great enthusiasm. They sent parcels to the ship with such comforts as knitted scarfs, mitts and Balaclavas also chocolates, sweets and cigarettes as well as letters to the crew telling them about their lives and their school. Their kindness and thoughtfulness was much appreciated by the ship's company and many wrote letters back to the children.

H.M.S. Seaham was a Bangor Class Minesweeper one of 51 of that Class commissioned for the Royal Navy though nine of these were given a transfer to the Royal Indian Navy, H.M.S. Hartlepool and H.M.S. Middlesbrough being two of them.

At 180 feet long and a displacement of 675 tons with twin steam reciprocating engines H.M.S. Seaham was one of the larger Bangor's though with a draught of only nine feet she was not the most comfortable of ships in a heavy sea. She could roll with sea water up to the davits and there were times when crew quarters might have up to a foot of sea water surging from end to end.

Lieutenant Robert E. Brett, R.N.R. took command of the ship charged with the task of training his crew in a very short time scale into a first class team. Most of the Ratings had never been to sea before and had to learn the hard way to respect the sea and to love the sea. Much of the 'working up' was carried out with sailing's from Stornaway to Tobermory to Greenock.

On the 7 March 1942, H.M.S. Seaham left Greenock for West Africa with a recoaling stop at Ponta Delgarda, Portugal and leaving there on 15 March bound for Freetown, Sierra Leone. Target towing duties were carried out while she was making her way south along the West African coast.

Arriving in Durban at the beginning of May, some of the Ratings acquired a ships mascot in the form of a monkey. Named, Jenny, by the crew she lived quite happily aboard ship and though she was well fed she did like the occasional cigarette - to eat, lit or otherwise.

In the company of H.M.S. Boston and H.M.S. Whitehaven the ship continued to Mombasa and then on to the Suez Canal and into the Mediterranean to join the Mediterranean Fleet. Their work now consisted of escort duties out of Alexandria bringing in supply ships with munitions and equipment for the 8th Army in Libya. 'Seaham' with 'Boston was ordered to join the eastern section of a two part convoy code named 'Vigorous'. This convoy had to turn back after concentrated attacks by aircraft and U-boats in which H.M.S. Newcastle suffered some damage.

The ship's mascot, Jenny, did her bit during these sorties. She would jump up and down and create a din as aircraft approached long before anyone else had heard them. This behaviour had the men ready for action stations in very good time.

The main job, and that for which she was best equipped, was sweeping the coast for mines and for several weeks this potentially dangerous work was carried out between Mersah Matruh and Alexandria in the company of 'Boston' and 'Whitehaven'.

In December 1942, while again on escort duty, 'Seaham' was shot up by an aircraft and also sustained slight damage from a near miss when the aircraft attacked a convoy.

While escorting an empty tanker back to Alexandria in February 1943, 'Seaham', accompanied by the Corvette H.M.S. Snapdragon, was attacked by German aircraft. The tanker and the escorting Corvette received direct hits and were lost. Thirty five men of the 'Snapdragon's' crew were lost but one of the survivors, 'Jimmy' James of Southampton, after the war, found and corresponded with the pilot of the aircraft that had sunk his ship. There was no animosity; it was war.

This same aircraft attacked 'Seaham' but its bombs missed so it strafed her with cannon fire but eventually gave up and returned to base.

By the beginning of May 1943 'Seaham' was at Malta with more duties of sweeping the entrance to Grand Harbour for a much needed supply convoy to reach the inhabitants of Malta. The 14th Mine Sweeping Flotilla, of which 'Seaham was one, now prepared for the next big showdown, the invasion of Sicily, Operation 'Husky'.

On July 9 the 14th MSF together with the 13th MSF set off for the shores of Sicily to sweep before the landings of troops took place. As darkness fell American aircraft towing gliders flew over the flotilla but a number were cast off to early and did not make it to land at Avola. By daybreak there were over a thousand ships of all sizes in this sector and it was not long before the Lufrwaffe attacked in force. Some ships were sunk as 'Seaham' and the 14 MSF swept 'Acid' sector that day and patrolled in the hours of darkness.

On 12 July shore batteries rained heavy fire on 'Seaham', 'Boston', 'Poole' and 'Cromarty' as they swept into Augusta. Discretion was the better part of valour and Lt. Cdr. Charles (Bunty) Palmer who was in command of this group decided that the four minesweepers should withdraw to seaward of the cruisers which had by this time arrived to set up a bombardment. The four minsweepers began an asdic sweep parallel with the warships in order to give protection from submarines.

Shortly, contact was made with submarines and depth charges were dropped but it was with some surprise to the men on deck when a submarine surfaced dead ahead and beam on about four hundred yards off. It brought about a hail of gunfire from 'Seaham'. Her three inch gun found its mark on the conning tower probably destroying the periscope. As quickly as it had surfaced the submarine dived again only to resurface a few moments later. 'Boston also opened fire with her three inch gun but as she was in line with 'Seaham' the danger was soon realised. Seaham was ordered to ram the submarine but before this action could be carried out the submarine surrendered which was just as well as a ramming action would

Chapter 8,

have seriously damage 'Seaham'. On the bridge at this time and at the wheel was Paul Jasper of Worthing who was glad that the ramming order was rescinded for down in the engine room were shipmates Leading Stoker Joe Bragger of Sheffield and Leading Stoker Bert Gleave of Blackpool.

Commander Brett ordered a boarding party to take over the submarine 'Bronzo'. The boarding party was lead by the 1st Officer, Lt. 'Dumbo' Bolton armed with a service revolver. On securing the 'Bronzo' he found that the captain, Cesare Boldini, had been mortally wounded. Nine of the 'Bronzo's' crew died in this action and thirty six survived among them Petty Officer (Electrician) Rudolfo Borrani, Dist. D'onore., of Stiava (Lucca).

As the First Officer of the 'Bronzo' surrendered his vessel to Lt. Bolton 'Seaham had picked up another asdic sounding of a submarine and began to track away from their captured sub to the chagrin of Lt. Bolton. However, 'Seaham' returned a short time later and took the 'Bronzo' in tow. Aboard 'Seaham' the 1st Officer of 'Bronzo' was able to tell Commander Brett that they did not know that Syracuse had been taken by the Allies and they thought that they were surfacing among friendly vessels.

In Syracuse harbour 'Seaham's' crew were able to spend a short respite in the warm sunshine after the excitement of the day. A strange sight was observed in the town as many Lire banknotes were blowing about in the streets.

The next big assignment for 'Seaham' was the sweeping of the Straits of Bonifacio in the company of 'Cromarty', 'Poole' and 'Boston'. The clearing of the Straits was important for a future invasion of the South of France, still in German hands. All the sea mines that were available had been dumped in these waters and some were just three or four feet under the surface. On 23 October, Commander 'Bunty' Palmer in Cromarty ordered shallow draught vessels to lead the sweep followed by the Fleet Sweepers. There was only one shallow boat available, an Italian sweeper which lead 'Cromarty' and the three other sweepers out of Maddalena.

The Italian vessel cut a mine and as it bobbed to the surface 'Cromart' tried to avoid it but in vain. Cromarty was wrecked and sank within a minute. Commander 'Bunty' Palmer of New Zealand survived but was badly wounded.

The 14th Fleet was relieved by the 13th Fleet and 'Seaham' returned to Malta for the last time before leaving the Mediterranean on her way home. Whilst making her way through the Bay of Biscay on the 29 December, 1943 there was further drama. The German blockade runner 'Alsterufer' had been sunk by Allied aircraft and there were 62 survivors from this ship picked up by 'Seaham' and brought in to Falmouth on 2 January, 1944. The ship was now in need of repairs throughout January and February.

In the spring of 1944, two young ratings from H.M.S. Seaham visited the Seaham High Colliery School to talk to the children about their ship. The boys wanted to know such things as, 'how many guns has she got, has she shot down any German planes etc., etc.' These shy, unasuming sailor lads gave what information was alowed to be given as the teacher left the room so that they would not be inhibited. At last the pupils were able to meet their heroes face to face.

Under the Plymouth Command what was left of the 14th MSF, the 'Romney', 'Boston' and 'Seaham' had been employed in minesweeping the English Channel and approaches to British ports. The time was fast moving towards the biggest event of the war for the minesweepers - Operation 'Neptune' which was the code name for the Naval operation in the 'Overlord' invasion of Europe.

This massive operation saw a total of 10 Mine Sweeper Flotillas taking part in clearing the mines to the approaches to the Normandy beaches. 'Seaham's' involvement was in sweeping the Number 2 channel leading in to 'Utah' Beach of the Western Task Force. Of course the shore batteries put up a fierce barrage but were thwarted to some extent by smoke screens set up by the destroyers.

Accompanying the Fleet Sweepers were the Danlayers, many of these were converted trawlers and drifters, and they would follow the sweepers in order to lay out channels for the invasion forces. At one point the Senior Officer of the Danlayers, Lt. Commander Croom-Johnson R.N.V.R. in 'Peterhead' kept close in behind 'Seaham' and went wherever she went. The problem was that, unknown to Croom-Johnson, 'Seaham had a mine caught up in her sweep and was desperately trying to lose it. All in all the D-Day landings were successful and in no small measure to the bravery and dedication to the task of the little ships such and H.M.S. Seaham.

Over the next months there was much experimentation carried out by 'Seaham' to try to overcome the problems of the pressure mines or 'Oyster mines'. This entailed towing 'egg-crates' a box like contraption which rather resembled an egg crate. However, these operations were not very successful.

Lieutenant Commander Robert E. Brett D.S.O., D.S.C. R.D. R.N.R. left the ship later in 1944 and took up command of the Harwich Naval Base. The ships company made a presentation to Bob Brett of a silver cigarette box inscribed:-

> 'Presented by the ships company in appreciation of 3 years
> devoted and skilful leadership.'

The size of the box was designed to take the standard cigarette well known to servicemen at that time.

'Seaham's' new Captain was Lieutenant Commander D.R. Hopking D.S.C. R.N.V.R. a jovial man who sported a full beard. He commanded his ship in sweeping duties along the French, Belgian and Dutch coasts as the Allies moved through Europe.

As war came to a close the M.P. for Seaham, Mr Emanuel Shinwell began to make inquiries at the Admiralty as to whether H.M.S. Seaham might be allowed to visit the town. Permission was of course granted and on 9 November 1945, for 'Thanksgiving Week', she

Chapter 8,

steamed proudly into Seaham Harbour. The ship was thrown open to the public and children visiting received a small chocolate bar. They clambered into every small chamber, up stairways, gun positions, mess decks etc. Officers were showing smartly dressed young ladies around the ship and the crew were chatting happily to everyone who came on board.

On the Friday of that week the Officers and men of H.M.S. Seaham were entertained to dinner by the Seaham Savings Committee in the British Restaurant in Adelaide Row. In proposing the toast, 'H.M.S. Seaham' Counc. H.F. Lee, Chairman of the Committee, extended a hearty welcome to the ships company and said that because the ship bore the name of Seaham this had created a remarkable link of intimacy and friendship which would never be forgotten.

In replying, Lt. Commander Hopking thanked the people of Seaham for their wonderful hospitality. He made a point of mentioning the pupils of Seaham High Colliery School who had sent many parcels to the ship over the years. He thanked Mr Shinwell for arranging the visit to Seaham and he congratulated the Savings Committee in passing their target of £55,000 in the last savings drive. There had been a collection on board the ship throughout the week which had so far raised £32.

Stoker Ainge of H.M.S. Seaham gave the toast, 'The people of Seaham.'

From the end of November 'Seaham' was allocated to Fisheries Protection duties in the North Sea and carried out these patrolling duties for the rest of the year and into 1946. With the war over and men returning home to take up their lives where they had left off in 1939 there were more ships in the Royal Navy than men to man them. It was decided that H.M.S. Seaham was no longer require and she was subsequently sold to the Rangoon Port Commissioners, Burma in 1947. There she was converted to the role of pilot cutter and tender and she was renamed 'Chinthe' meaning 'Lion', for a lion she was.

The final irony came in 1948, while working out of Rangoon Harbour and going about her peaceful endeavours. Our little ship struck a mine and sank. She lies there today, perhaps dreaming of her glorious days and of the men who had loved her.

Postscript

As I have said earlier, Bill Bulmer of Stotfold Farm brought the matter of the crashed aircraft to the fore when I was looking for a date for this incident. He was not sure about the date though he had been involved with the search for the plane at the time. However, he decided to take a look through his crop rotation diary and there it was, 'Aircraft down 17 October, 1944.' With this information I was then able to find out more about the aircraft and her crew. So started many years of research into life in Seaham throughout the years 1939 - 1945.

The 'Apple Barrel Kid', Jack Salsman and pen-friend of Hiram Brass of Murton was not found but a letter from a Faye Salsman and her husband Jack had some interesting things to say. It seems that a number of the Salsman family came from Kings County, Nova Scotia which is the 'Apple Capital' of Eastern Canada. Faye tells me that her husband's grandfather and great grandfather were both coopers so it is entirely possible that Hiram's pen-friend is to be found in that family.

Tim Sheedy of Alberta, Canada though not in the best of health is still active and keenly interested in working with his computer. He described his visit to Murton with his then new wife as a wonderful experience. They met and made friends with so many people and he said that it was a great privilege to be 'adopted' by such kind and generous people. At the party held in their honour he remembers a piper playing them into the room and his wife was so overcome with emotion she was unable to speak. They had always hoped to revisit those kind people again but alas it was not to be.

The crew members of H.M.S. Seaham, Paul Jasper, Bert Gleave and Joe Bragger were found through 'Navy News'. Unfortunately Joe had suffered a mild stroke at that time but he was so enthusiastic about my enquiries of his ship that he wrote many pages using his left hand as his right hand had suffered some paralysis. He sent photographs and a fine ship's plaque of H.M.S. Seaham which now hangs in a place of honour in my home. Bert Gleave gave me much information on the ship and his comrades. However, it was not long after this that he decided to go and live with his son in South Africa.

Paul Jasper was also of great help to me and his friendly letters a joy to read. He was able to visit Seaham when Bill Brett, son of 'Seaham's' first captain, came to an official ceremony at the Council Offices in Seaham on 25 July, 1995. This was quite an emotional meeting between Bill and Paul, the only known survivor of the ship his father commanded. Bill, with his wife Mary Jo and his sister Pat attended the ceremony to present photographs and a silver cigarette box to the town. The cigarette box had been presented to his father, Robert E. Brett, by the crew of 'Seaham' and he always felt that if Bill should ever manage to visit Seaham then he would like the box to be presented to the town.

The ship's bell is in the care of 'Dumbo' Bolton's family and perhaps is the only tangible reminder of H.M.S. Seaham. One day it also might 'come home' to Seaham.

Bibliography

Hamlin	-	History of 20th Century Conflict
Bill Norman	-	Luftwaffe Over the North
Ripley and Pears	-	A North East Diary
Emanuel Shinwell	-	Conflict Without Malice
Ivan Way	-	Our Village
Jack Williams	-	Fleet Minesweepers at War
Mike Brown	-	A Child's War
Len Deighton	-	Battle of Britain
Other sources	-	'Quadrante' Sommergibili Italiani
		RAF Records in the PRO